PUZZLES
& BRAIN
TEASERS

FOR GARDENERS

PUZZLES
& BRAIN
TEASERS

FOR GARDENERS

*100 Quizzes and Games
for Plant Lovers*

SIMON AKEROYD
& DR GARETH MOORE

MITCHELL BEAZLEY

RHS Puzzles & Brain Teasers for Gardeners
Authors: Simon Akeroyd and Gareth Moore
First published in Great Britain in 2023
by Mitchell Beazley, an imprint of Octopus
Publishing Group Ltd, Carmelite House,
50 Victoria Embankment, London EC4Y 0DZ

www.octopusbooks.co.uk
An Hachette UK Company
www.hachette.co.uk

Published in association with the
Royal Horticultural Society
© 2023 Quarto Publishing plc

ISBN: 978-1-78472-9127

A CIP record of this book is available
from the British Library

Printed and bound in China

Mitchell Beazley Publisher: Alison Starling
Mitchell Beazley Editorial Assistant:
Jeannie Stanley
RHS Book Publishing Manager: Helen
Griffin
RHS Consultant Editor: Simon Maughan
RHS Head of Editorial: Tom Howard

Conceived, designed and produced by
The Bright Press, an imprint of
The Quarto Group.
1 Triptych Place, London SE1 9SH
United Kingdom
(0)20 7700 6700
www.Quarto.com

Design: Clare Barber

The Royal Horticultural Society is the
UK's leading gardening charity dedicated to
advancing horticulture and promoting good
gardening. Its charitable work includes
providing expert advice and information in
print, online and at its five major gardens
and annual shows, training gardeners of
every age, creating hands-on opportunities
for children to grow plants and sharing
research into plants, wildlife, wellbeing and
environmental issues affecting gardeners.

For more information visit www.rhs.org.uk
or call 020 3176 5800.

CONTENTS

How to Use This Book

This book offers you the chance to pit your horticultural wits against friends and family members or just to test your own grey matter. It is a great way of checking to see if you really do know your onions... or any alliums for that matter.

The chapters are arranged according to the following specialized subjects: kitchen gardening; horticultural heroes; wonderful wildlife; botany basics; plant identification; gardening techniques; gardens around the world; garden features and design; and tales from the potting shed. No matter what your level of gardening ability or horticultural knowledge, there are puzzles to suit both experienced and amateur gardeners. Some are simply multiple-choice or quick-fire rounds on specific subjects. Others ask you to identify plants from their pictures or from other clues. There are also mix-and-match style puzzles, where you have to link corresponding pairs or groups. Not all of the puzzles set out to test your knowledge as such. Thrown in for good measure are a handful of fun – sometimes challenging – brain teasers, spot the differences, dot to dots and logic problems, all with a horticultural theme.

The book is beautifully illustrated through-out but don't be deceived by the images – you may find some of them are purely decorative. To check whether you have successfully solved a puzzle or quiz, turn to the back of the book where you can find all of the answers.

KEY TO DIFFICULTY

❦ ❦ ❦ ❦ ❦

You will find a rough guide to the skill level required at the start of each puzzle – rated from one leaf for the easiest to five leaves for the most difficult.

Chapter One

KITCHEN GARDENING

What am I?

Can you guess what popular fruit or veg I am from the clues below? Score 10 points if you solve the puzzle with one clue and deduct a point for every additional clue that you need.

1. I belong to the *Rosaceae* family.

2. My tree produces flowers (pictured) early on in the growing season, and in cooler climates they can be prone to frost damage.

3. I became the state fruit of Georgia, USA, in 1995.

4. There is a stone at my centre.

5. Popular varieties include 'Rochester' and 'Peregrine'.

6. China is my biggest producer, with an annual production of 11 million tonnes, representing half the output of the entire world.

7. A popular alcoholic schnapps drink is made from the juice of my fruit.

8. My leaves are prone to getting a fungus that causes them to curl up.

9. My botanical name is *Prunus persica*.

10. I have a slightly furry skin and I am closely related to the smoother-skinned nectarine.

Answers: page 164

Four, but no more!

Imagine the grid below is a raised bed in which you wish to plant peas and carrots. Place either an 'X' to mark peas or an 'O' to mark carrots into each empty square so that no line of four or more Xs or Os is formed in any direction, including diagonally.

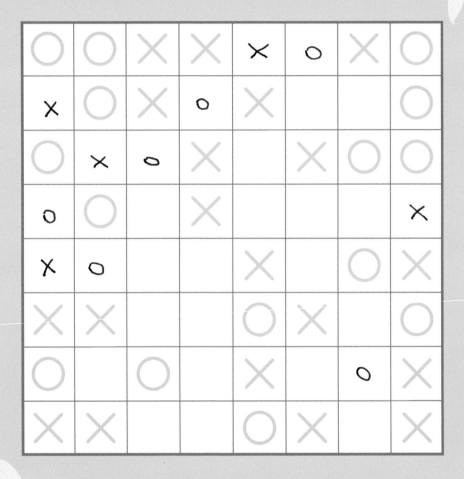

Answers: page 164

Fruit-filled still life

Below are the titles of six world-famous paintings featuring
popular fruit. Can you fill in the names of the missing fruit? If you
recognize the painting pictured, you'll be off to a good start!

1. *Still Life with Lemons,* _ _ _ _ _ _ _ *and a Rose*
   (1633) by Francisco de Zurbarán

2. *Jar of* _ _ _ _ _ _ _ **(1866) by Claude Monet**

3. *The Meal,* **also known as** *The* _ _ _ _ _ _ _ **(1891)**
   by Paul Gauguin

4. *Basket of* _ _ _ _ _ _ **(c. 1893) by Paul Cézanne**

5. _ _ _ _ _ _ _ _ _ _ _ **(1908)**
   by John Singer Sargent

6. *Still Life with Apples, Pears,* _ _ _ _ _ _ *and Grapes*
   (1887) by Vincent Van Gogh

Planting seeds

Can you plant 16 pumpkin seeds in this grid, spacing them out so that there is room for the vines to grow? To do this, make sure that each row, column and outlined region contains exactly two seeds. You must also not place seeds in touching squares – not even diagonally.

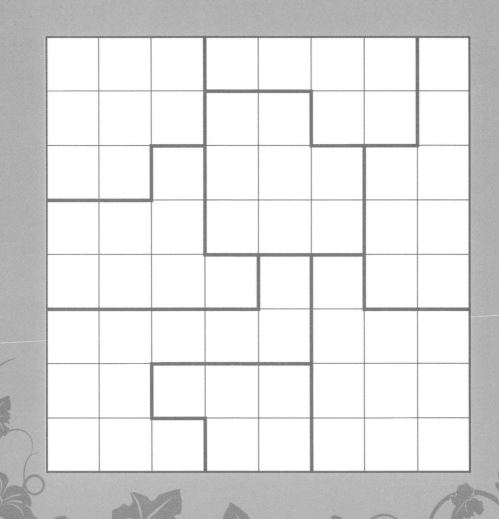

Gourmet variety

Below are lists of fruit and veg varieties. For each list, see if you can name the type of fruit or veg. To help you, one of each is pictured as a clue, but not in the right order!

A.

PLANT VARIETIES

1. 'Blue Tit', 'Opal', 'Victoria'

2. 'Worcester Pearmain', 'Discovery', 'Howgate Wonder'

3. 'Gardener's Delight', 'Sungold', 'Marmande'

4. 'Maris Piper', 'Charlotte', 'Pink Fir Apple'

5. 'Autumn King', 'Nantes 2', 'Rainbow'

6. 'Gladiator', 'Albion', 'Tender and True'

7. 'Boltardy', 'Chioggia', 'Morello'

8. 'Scarlet Emperor', 'Painted Lady', 'White Lady'

9. 'Hurst Green Shaft', 'Kelvedon Wonder', 'Alderman'

10. 'Little Gem', 'Iceberg', 'Cos'

11. 'Timperley Early', 'Victoria', 'Fulton's Strawberry Surprise'

12. 'Trafalgar', 'Brodie', 'Crispus'

B.

C.

D.

E.

F.

G.

H.

I.

J.

K.

L.

Answers: page 164

Anagrams: Mixed salad

The names of some popular fruit and veg salad ingredients have been jumbled up. Can you unscramble them to discover what they are?

1. SPINRAP
2. HAIRBLOK
3. BURLESS PORTUS
4. TROCAR
5. RHRCEY
6. AUAVG
7. TIMN
8. NEFELN
9. IHLICL
10. OTAPOT
11. YARSOREM
12. EOTBETOR
13. MYTHE
14. NABAAN
15. NORAEG

Answers: page 165

Edible parts

Which parts of the following vegetables do we actually eat?
Write the number of each listed vegetable above the correct part
of the plant, so that each group has five vegetables in total.

VEGETABLES

1. Artichoke
2. Potato
3. Kale
4. Cauliflower
5. Spinach
6. Carrot
7. Borage
8. Sweet potato

9. Broccoli
10. Cabbage
11. Rocket
12. Beetroot
13. Nasturtium
14. Parsnip
15. Lettuce

LEAF

ROOT/TUBER

FLOWER

Answers: page 165

Shapely edibles

Can you identify these quirky-looking
gourmet vegetables that you may find
growing in a kitchen garden? Link each of
the listed vegetables with its photo.

A.

B.

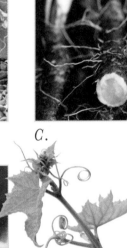

C.

D.

E.

F.

VEGETABLES

1. Kohlrabi
2. Celeriac
3. Okra
4. Amaranthus
5. Cardoon
6. Seakale

7. Asparagus
8. Broad bean
9. Sweet potato
10. Lemongrass
11. Luffa
12. Black salsify

G.

H.

I.

J.

K.

L.

Answers: page 165

Quick quiz: Know your onions

Answer these quick-fire questions to test
your fruit, veg and herb knowledge.

1. Which common vegetables, sometimes used to top a pie, would you expect to 'chit' before planting and 'earth up' as they started growing?

2. Which herb has two variations, often known as flat or curly leaved?

3. Which fruit or veg pictured opposite has 'determinate' and 'indeterminate' types, and produces varieties that include beefsteak, tumbling and cherry?

4. Which red or pink vegetable is often 'forced' in the dark to produce sweet, succulent stems in early spring?

5. What fruit is known botanically as *Ribes uva-crispa*?

6. One insect in particular is associated with the pollination of some cultivars of fig tree so they can produce fruit. What insect is it?

7. What colour is the kale known as 'Cavolo Nero'?

8. What type of fruit-bearing woody climber is sometimes trained on a system known as Geneva double curtains or double guyot?

9. What root vegetable is typically purple but also has yellow or golden varieties?

10. 'Romanesco' is a hybrid vegetable that looks like a cross between which two other vegetables?

11. Russian and French are two common types of what aromatic herb?

12. What type of fruit or vegetable is the 'Carolina Reaper'?

Answers: page 165

Dish of the day

Here's a quiz to tantalize your taste buds, as well as tax those grey
– or should we say green – cells of yours. Can you match each
vegetable, fruit or herb ingredient with the dish it features in?

INGREDIENTS

1. Aubergine
2. Tomato
3. Chickpea
4. Avocado
5. Basil
6. Potato
7. Coffee beans
8. Coconut
9. Almond
10. Onion
11. Chamomile
12. Cocoa

RECIPE

A. Korma
B. Pesto
C. Cappuccino
D. Ketchup
E. Guacamole
F. Moussaka
G. Bhaji
H. Mole sauce
I. Rösti
J. Falafel
K. Frangipane
L. Tea

Answers: page 165

Crop rotation

It is time to rotate your crops! But first you need to categorize your vegetables into family groups with similar characteristics. Write the number of each listed vegetable below each group or family name, so that each one has four vegetables in total.

VEGETABLES

1. Broccoli
2. Carrot
3. Marrow
4. Brussel sprout
5. Broad bean
6. Cauliflower
7. Sugar snap
8. Chive
9. Celery
10. Shallot
11. Runner bean
12. Spring onion
13. Leek
14. Mangetout
15. Courgette
16. Kale
17. Pumpkin
18. Parsnip
19. Cucumber
20. Radish

PLOTS

A. Brassicas

B. Legumes

C. Onions

D. Cucurbits

E. Roots

Answers: page 166

Hanjie: Shading by numbers

Reveal a vegetable in the grid by shading some squares according to the given clue numbers. The clues provide, in reading order from left to right or top to bottom, the length of every run of consecutive shaded squares in each row and column. There must be a gap of at least one empty square between each run of shaded squares in the same row or column.

SOLVING THE PUZZLE

Before you start, take a look at this example solved puzzle to make sure you understand the rules. To get started, look for rows or columns where there is only one possible solution, as in the bottom row in this example. When solving, marking squares you know to be empty with an 'x' will help you make further deductions.

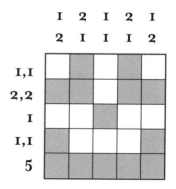

Name of vegetable _ U _ _ _ _ _ U _ _ _ U _ _ _

Multiple-choice: Grow your own

Test your growing knowledge with the following questions.

1. What herb is also referred to as cilantro?
a) Parsley
b) Coriander
c) Thyme
d) Dill

2. A garden system for collecting rainwater is called a water . . .?
a) Bottom
b) Brick
c) Bucket
d) Butt

3. What is the name for a low, portable protective cover used to protect plants?
a) Trellis
b) Cloche
c) Planter
d) Trough

4. Which one of these is not a root vegetable?
a) Potato
b) Parsnip
c) Kale
d) Skirret

5. Which one of the following crops is botanically classed as a fruit?
a) Courgette
b) Rhubarb
c) Swede
d) Kohlrabi

6. What are the tender young shoots of asparagus commonly known as?
a) Javelins
b) Spears
c) Swords
d) Lances

7. What type of citrus is a variety called 'Meyer'?
a) Lemon
b) Tangerine
c) Grapefruit
d) Satsuma

8. A shallow trench for sowing seeds into it is known as a what?
a) Screw
b) Bolt
c) Drill
d) Spanner

9. Which one of the following is botanically a vegetable?
a) Tomato
b) Rhubarb
c) Cucumber
d) Marrow

10. What are the offshoots of strawberries called?
a) Joggers
b) Runners
c) Sprinters
d) Ramblers

11. The edible parts of the root system of the potato are correctly known as what?
a) Tubers
b) Stolons
c) Corms
d) Bulbs

12. NPK is often seen written on packets of plant fertilizers. What does NPK stand for?
a) Nitrogen, phosphorus, potassium
b) Nitrogen, potassium, krypton
c) Nickel, plutonium, phosphorus
d) Nickel, plutonium, krypton

Answers: page 166

Chapter Two
HORTICULTURAL HEROES

Recommended reading

Can you fill in the missing words to reveal some of history's most influential gardening books?

1. _ _ _ _ _ _ _ _ *Commoda* by Pietro Crescenzi (1490–95)

2. *Instructions in Gardening for* _ _ _ _ _ _
by Jane C Loudon (1834)

3. *The American* _ _ _ _ _ _ _ by William Cobbett (1821)

4. *The* _ _ _ _ *Garden* by William Robinson (1870)

5. *Wall and* _ _ _ _ _ *Gardens* by Gertrude Jekyll (1901)

6. *We made a* _ _ _ _ _ _ by Margery Fish (1956)

7. *The* _ _ _ _ *-Tempered Garden* by Christopher Lloyd (1970)

8. *The* _ _ _ *Garden* by Beth Chatto (1978)

9. *The* _ _ _ _ _ _ _ _ _ _ *of a Gardener* by Russell Page (1994)

10. *The* _ _ _ _ _ by Anna Pavord (1999)

Answers: page 167

Taxonomic triangles

Copy the letters from each of the loose triangular pieces onto an empty triangle in the grid, so that every row of letters spells out the solution to a taxonomic clue listed below. None of the triangles should be rotated. To help you out, the answer to Row 2 is pictured here.

TAXONOMIC CLUES

- Row 1 (top): Maple genus
- Row 2: Beech genus
- Row 3: Plant kingdom
- Row 4: Bean family
- Row 5: Sunflower genus
- Row 6: Daffodil order

Who am I?

Can you figure out which horticultural hero I am from the past?
How many clues will it take you to work it out? Score 10 points
if you can figure it out with just one clue, and deduct one
point for every extra one you need.

1. I was born in the north of England, in a village called Kirkharle.

2. I married a lady called Bridget Wayet (affectionately called Biddy) and had eight children.

3. My first landscape commission was the creation of a lake in the park at Kiddington Hall, Oxfordshire.

4. I was appointed head gardener at Stowe in Buckingham at the age of 26.

5. I share my first name with one of King Arthur's Knights of the Round Table.

6. I'm considered to be one of the most influential landscape gardeners in British history and led the way in the English Landscape Movement.

7. I planted what is now the oldest and largest grapevine in the world at Hampton Court Palace.

8. I designed more than 170 gardens including Sheffield Park, Gatton Park and Audley End. Can you guess the names of the four parks I designed on the opposite page?

9. My surname is a colour.

10. I was given a nickname because of my ability to see the potential of a garden and carry out the work competently.

Answers: page 167

At the movies

Gardening has been a central theme in a number of films
over the years. Can you match each film title to
the right image below?

FILMS

1. *Greenfingers* (2000)

2. *The Secret Garden* (1993)

3. *This Beautiful Fantastic* (2016)

4. *Serpent's Kiss* (1997)

5. *Dare to be Wild* (2015)

6. *A Little Chaos* (2014)

A.   *B.*   *C.*

D.   *E.*   *F.*

Answers: page 167

Famous gardeners

Place the surnames of these famous gardeners into the grid.
Write one letter per grid square so that each surname can be
read either across or down, crossword style.

Gardeners

- Alan **TITCHMARSH**
- 'Capability' **BROWN**
- Charles **DARWIN**
- Edwin Beard **BUDDING**
- Elizabeth **BANKS**
- Fanny **WILKINSON**
- Gertrude **JEKYLL**
- Helena Rutherfurd **ELY**
- Humphry **REPTON**
- Jane **WEBB**
- John Claudius **LOUDON**
- Joseph **PAXTON**

- Monty **DON**
- Mrs Francis **KING**
- Peter **COLLINSON**
- Pippa **GREENWOOD**
- Sylvia **CROWE**
- William **KENT**
- William **ROBINSON**

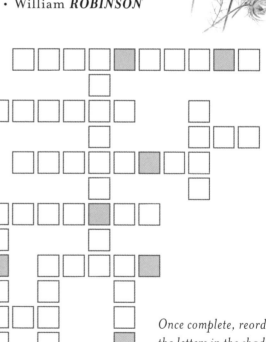

*Once complete, reorder
the letters in the shaded
squares to reveal the
name of a garden created
by Vita Sackville-West
and Harold Nicolson
in the early 1930s.*

Answers: page 168

Where in the world?

Many of the plants listed below have found their way into gardens across the globe. But do you know their places of origin? Match each plant not only to its photograph, but also to its native region in the world.

PLANTS

1. *Dahlia* sp.

2. *Pinus radiata*

3. *Wollemia nobilis*

4. *Amorphophallus titanum*

5. *Dracunculus vulgaris*

6. *Victoria amazonica*

7. *Agapanthus* sp.

8. *Araucaria araucana*

F

C

COUNTRIES OF ORIGIN

A. Southern Africa

B. Mediterranean

C. Central America

D. Sumatra, Indonesia

E. South America

F. Southwest North America

G. Central and southern Chile and western Argentina

H. Blue Mountains of Australia

E

G

I.

J.

K.

L.

B

D

A

H

M.

N.

O.

P.

Answers: page 168

Horticulturally named celebrities

Unscramble the following anagrams to find the names
of celebrities or bands with plant-themed names.
Number 9 on the list comes with a cryptic picture clue!

1. TAKE SHUB

2. ALLEH YERRB

3. SNUG N SORES

4. NOTES ORESS

5. TREBOR LANPT

6. OBB WORLDEFEW

7. GALLINE ANSLOW

8. NESA NEBA

9. REGING OGRRES

10. HET NEARSCRIBER

ZINGIBER OFFICINALE

Answers: page 168

Brick by brick

Complete this pyramid by writing a number in each
empty brick, so that each brick contains a value equal
to the sum of the two bricks immediately beneath it.
Once complete, the shaded brick will reveal the
year in which 'Capability' Brown became
Master Gardener at Hampton Court Palace.

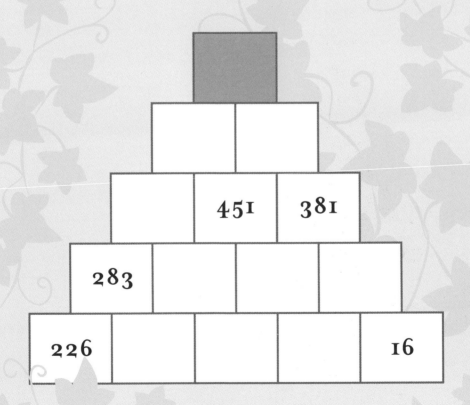

Mix and match: Plant hunters

In the past, plant hunters travelled far and wide in their quest to learn about plants in far-flung countries. Match each of the following plant-hunting facts to its plant hunter. To help you out, both the facts and their hunters have been given dates, but this doesn't make it all plain sailing!

PLANT-HUNTING FACTS

1. After falling into a bull pit in Hawaii, this plant hunter was gored to death by a bull (1834).

2. Disguising themselves as a Chinese tea merchant/plantation worker, they risked being captured as a spy, in order to smuggle tea plants out of the country (1850s).

MONKEY PUZZLE TREE

3. This intrepid plant hunter was crushed by an avalanche of rocks whilst exploring the Min area of China. The incident left him with a limp for the rest of his life (1910).

4. This botanist took seeds of the giant sequoia from California to Britain, where the tree became a sensation among wealthy Victorians. In Britain, the tree was named *Wellingtonia gigantea* (1853).

5. Which hunter covered more than 9,650km (6,000 miles) on a five-year exploration of Central and South America? Travelling on horseback, on foot and by canoe, at times they had just wild cacao beans and river water for sustenance (1799–1804).

A PLATE FROM JOSEPH BANKS' *FLORILEGIUM*

PLANT HUNTERS

A. Marianne North
(1830–90)

B. David Douglas
(1799–1834)

C. Frank Kingdon-Ward
(1885–1958)

D. William Lobb
(1809–64)

E. Joseph Banks
(1743–1820)

F. Alexander von Humboldt
(1769–1859)

G. Robert Fortune
(1812–80)

H. Reginald Farrer
(1880–1920)

I. Ernest Wilson
(1876–1930)

J. Archibald Menzies
(1754–1842)

6. This hunter sailed on the *Endeavour* to South America, New Zealand and Australia. Later, he became president of the Royal Horticultural Society, a post he held for 40 years (1768).

7. This plant hunter discovered *Geranium farreri* in the Min mountains of upper Burma, but died there six years later of diphtheria (1914).

8. Known for creating exquisite botanical drawings, and particularly for painting plants in their natural settings, which plant hunter defied the conventions of the age to travel alone to wild and far-flung places (1870s–80s)?

9. This Scotsman is credited with having introduced the quirky looking monkey puzzle tree to England, having brought seeds back from Chile (1795).

10. As well as being a plant hunter and botanist, this explorer also served as a spy for the British India Office (1935).

Answers: page 169

A CONIFER FOREST

WORDS TO SEARCH FOR

- *Abies amabilis*
- *Abies grandis*
- *Abies procera*
- *Abies venusta*
- *Pinus contorta*
- *Pinus coulteri*
- *Pinus lambertiana*
- *Pinus monticola*
- *Pinus ponderosa*
- *Pinus radiata*
- *Pinus sabiniana*
- *Picea sitchensis*
- *Pseudotsuga menziesii*
- *Tsuga heterophylla*

PINUS SYLVESTRIS

Word search: Evergreens and conifers

Find these North American evergreens and conifers in the puzzle below.
They can run vertically or horizontally in any direction. They all found
their way to Europe, thanks to prolific Victorian plant collector David
Douglas. For an extra point, which of the listed trees is more commonly
known as the Douglas fir?

```
I  H  U  P  I  N  U  S  S  A  B  I  N  I  A  N  A  C  I  K
I  B  N  M  I  O  U  H  P  T  E  F  P  R  Y  Y  L  R  W  K
S  O  F  Q  R  K  O  P  P  A  A  T  I  A  T  J  O  F  X  O
E  G  K  A  E  A  F  I  J  I  I  V  N  S  S  L  C  R  P  L
I  D  T  G  T  T  P  N  Q  D  I  U  U  O  U  V  I  P  U  M
Z  A  Y  S  L  S  D  U  Q  A  B  L  S  R  G  T  T  S  W  V
N  B  K  T  U  U  L  S  V  R  R  F  C  E  A  T  N  I  N  C
E  I  M  Q  O  N  A  L  I  S  X  C  O  D  H  K  O  S  P  C
M  E  T  D  C  E  B  A  T  U  X  W  N  N  E  Q  M  N  C  C
A  S  Q  B  S  V  I  M  F  N  Q  U  T  O  T  K  S  E  D  Q
G  A  C  W  U  S  E  B  Q  I  U  M  O  P  E  E  U  H  N  Y
U  M  L  N  N  E  S  E  P  P  D  D  R  S  R  D  N  C  E  I
S  A  S  X  I  I  P  R  U  V  V  X  T  U  O  W  I  T  X  Y
T  B  E  F  P  B  R  T  J  Z  U  U  A  N  E  P  E  P  I  B  U
O  I  L  D  M  A  O  I  U  J  Q  K  C  I  H  G  D  S  D  U
D  L  F  S  U  P  C  A  L  F  X  H  G  P  Y  A  O  A  B  Y
U  I  A  F  S  S  E  N  I  C  Z  S  G  M  L  D  D  E  M  C
E  S  I  Y  A  P  R  A  A  U  B  L  W  I  L  I  F  C  G  N
S  R  C  I  H  B  A  V  X  R  I  A  A  W  A  Q  D  I  N  H
P  M  A  X  A  B  I  E  S  G  R  A  N  D  I  S  N  P  F  I
```

Chapter Three

WONDERFUL WILDLIFE

What am I?

Can you guess what kind of garden visitor I am from the clues below? Score 12 points if you solve the puzzle with one clue and deduct a point for every additional clue that you need.

1. I am a bird of flight.

2. I am found widely throughout North and South America, Europe, Asia and Africa.

3. There are about 230 species of my type in the world.

4. My scientific family name is *Picidae*.

5. Some of my family members are known as wrynecks and sapsuckers.

6. I can be found in a variety of habitats, but I am most commonly found in deciduous woodlands.

7. The collective noun for my type of bird is a 'descent'.

8. My largest species type is the imperial.

9. My smallest species type is the piculet.

10. Commonly seen species in the UK and Europe include the great spotted and lesser spotted.

11. I have a strong, sharp beak and a barbed tongue.

12. I use my beak to bore holes into wood and extract insects to feed on.

Answers: page 170

Pollination game

Link each of these pollinators with a
flower by drawing horizontal and vertical lines
to join them into pairs, so that each pair
contains one flower and one pollinator.
Lines cannot cross either one another or any
flower/pollinator. All pollinators and flowers
must be used in exactly one pair.

Multiple-choice: Garden visitors

All kinds of creatures, large and small, visit our gardens.
Test your knowledge of the animals you might expect to see
with these multiple-choice questions.

1. A codling moth is often found as a 'maggot' in which popular garden fruit?
a) Apple
b) Cherry
c) Peach
d) Lemon

2. *Otiorhynchus sulcatus* is a frequent garden visitor. What is it more commonly known as?
a) Pigeon
b) Vine weevil
c) Tortrix moth
d) Mealy bug

3. Which one of the following animals lives in a den?
a) Rabbit
b) Badger
c) Hare
d) Fox

4. Which one of the following is not a type of deer?
a) Fallow
b) Roe
c) Stow
d) Muntjac

5. Which of the four listed birds does not belong to the carrion (crow) family?
a) Raven
b) Rook
c) Blackbird
d) Jay

6. Which winged insects are gardeners trying to deter when they place grease bands around the trunks of apple trees?
a) Spring moth
b) Summer moth
c) Autumn moth
d) Winter moth

Answers: page 170

Mix and match: **Plant eaters**

Match the damage on each of the following plants
with the creature that might have caused it.

CREATURES

1. Deer
2. Vine weevil (adult)
3. Thrips
4. Box tree caterpillar

5. Glasshouse red spider mite
6. Bean gall sawfly
7. Gooseberry sawfly
8. Currant blister aphid

A. B. C. D.

E. F. G. H.

Answers: page 170

Wildlife wordoku

Reveal some wildlife that might be found in your garden by placing A, B, E, F, L, R, T, U or Y into each empty square, so that no letter repeats in any row, column or bold-lined 3 x 3 box. Once solved, the name of the wildlife can be read down the shaded diagonal.

					Y			T
A			B				R	
	R			L	U	Y		
		E				B		
L	A						Y	R
		U				A		
		R	E	B			T	
	F				T			A
U			F					

Identity parade: Brilliantly beautiful butterflies

Take a look at the following butterfly photographs and see if you know the common name for each type. A few of the letters in their names have been given to help you out.

1.

2.

3.

4.

5.

6.

1. _ E _ / A _ M _ R _ _
2. _ U _ L _ / _ M P _ R _ R
3. _ P _ C _ L _ D / W _ O _
4. _ M L _ / _ O R _ O _ _ E _ H _ _ L
5. _ O _ _ A
6. _ R _ M S _ O _ E

Answers: page 171

True or false?: Busy bees

Fingers on buzzers! Which of these facts about
honey bees are true and which are false?

1. There is only one female in a colony
of bees, and that is the queen.

2. Male bees are called drones
and do not sting.

3. There can be around 60,000
bees in a full colony during the
summer months.

4. Honey bees are more closely
related to earwigs than they are
to bumble bees.

5. One of the most popular types
of beehive, called a WBC beehive,
is named after British beekeeper
William Broughton Carr.

6. Beekeepers use a 'smoker' because
it sends bees to sleep before they open
the hive.

7. Keeping bees has been made more
difficult in recent years due to a
parasitic mite called Varroa.

8. The Asian hornet and the honey
bee have a symbiotic relationship,
whereby they help each other survive
by exchanging food.

9. Honey is predominately made from
pollen collected from flowers.

10. The main purpose of a 'hive tool'
is for a beekeeper to swat aggressive
bees away.

Answers: page 171

Hanjie: Shading by numbers

Reveal a garden visitor in the grid by shading some squares according to the given clue numbers. The clues provide, in reading order from left to right or top to bottom, the length of every run of consecutive shaded squares in each row and column. There must be a gap of at least one empty square between each run of shaded squares in the same row or column. For further help in solving the puzzle, turn to page 24.

PICTURE CLUES

1. There are more than 6,000 species of this animal worldwide.

2. It is amphibious and likes to spend time in freshwater ponds.

3. It can range from 1cm (½in) to 38cm (15in) in size.

4. Having long legs, it can leap more than 20 times its body length.

5. The name of the visitor is given opposite, with blanks for you to fill in.

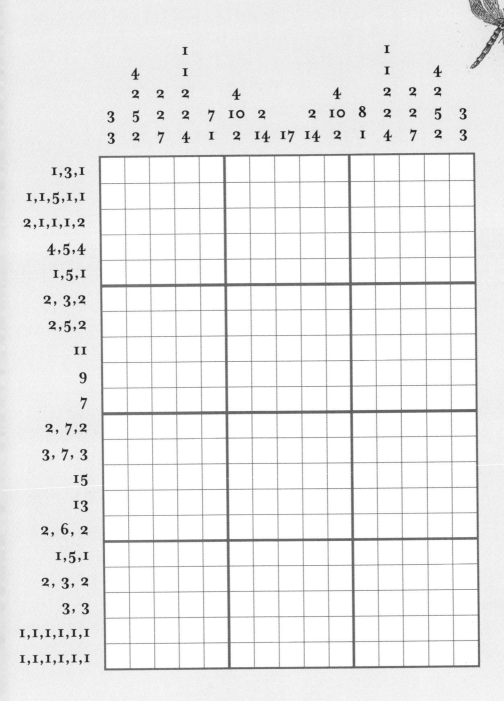

Name of visitor: _ _ O _

Bird-spotting

If you are very lucky, you may spot a bird of prey, either in your garden or circling in the sky above you in a park or in the open countryside. Can you match the names of the birds on the list below to their images?

BIRDS OF PREY

1. Buzzard

2. Red-tailed hawk

3. Merlin

4. Sparrowhawk

5. Kestrel

6. Great horned owl

7. Peregrine falcon

8. Barn owl

A.

B.

C.

D.

E.

F.

G.

H.

Dormouse quest

This puzzle works like a minesweeper, but instead of mines, you are looking for hibernating dormice! The numbers in some of the squares reveal the total count of dormice in touching squares – including diagonally. No more than one dormouse may be placed per square, and they cannot be hiding in numbered squares.

	I	2		2	3	
2				2		
			I		6	
		2	I			
I			I	2		3
I			2		2	
	2		2			I

Anagrams: Cryptic critters

Reorganize the letters of the anagrams below to reveal
the names of some of the critters you might see
passing through your garden.

1. DER RIDESP TIME　　5. TONEMEDA

2. NIEV VIEWEL　　6. ANILS

3. INGCOLD THOM　　7. RIAWEG

4. LOWLOY DIPAH　　8. XEROPHALLY

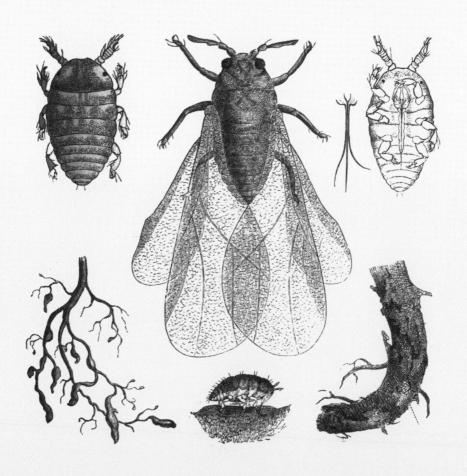

Spot the difference

Below is a picture of an idyllic woodland scene. Can you spot five differences between the two images?

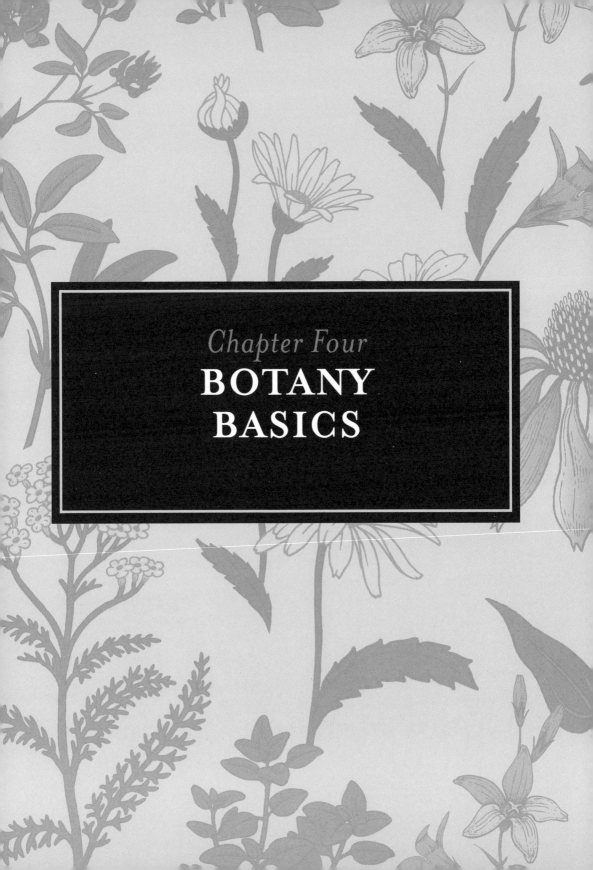

Chapter Four
BOTANY BASICS

Flower power

Below are six plants that favour an acidic soil. See if you can identify each of them just from their flowers.

THE PLANTS

1. Heather

2. Pieris

3. Camellia

4. Enkianthus

5. Rhododendron

6. Vaccinium

A.

B.

C.

D.

E.

F.

Answers: page 173

Climbing vines

Can you find the genus of ivy, *Hedera*, written among these
letter-strewn climbing vines? Start on any leaf you like and then
follow lines to touching leaves, so that each leaf visited in turn
spells out the word. No leaf can be revisited.

H	D		E	R		H	E	A
	D	E		D	E		E	D
E		H	D	D		H	E		H
	R	E		E		D		E
E		E	H	E	D		E	D
	H	A		D	E	E		H
E		A	R	E	E		H	A
	E		E	H	D		H	R
H		E	R	D		E	E	H
	A	E		E	D		H	H
E		A	D	R		H	D	H
	H	E		R	H		D	E
H	D		E	R	H		A	A

Fun with fungi

Identify these eight fungi from their photos. They can be found in American, European and Asian woodlands.

THE FUNGI

1. Oyster mushroom
(*Pleurotus ostreatus*)

2. Jelly ear
(*Auricularia auricula-judae*)

3. Giant puffball
(*Calvatia gigantea*)

4. Porcini
(*Boletus edulis*)

5. Chanterelle
(*Cantharellus cibarius*)

6. Razor strop
(*Fomitopsis betulina*)

7. Shaggy inkcap
(*Coprinus comatus*)

8. Fly agaric
(*Amanita muscaria*)

A.

B.

C.

D.

E.

F.

G.

H.

Answers: page 173

Taxonomic teaser

In the 18th century, Swedish botanist Carl Linnaeus created a hierarchy of natural living things, including plants. Scientists continue to use it to this day. See if you can place the categories in the correct order.

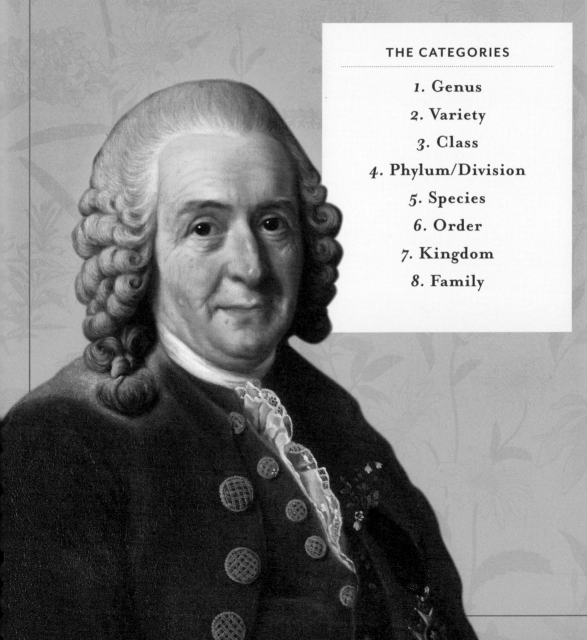

THE CATEGORIES

1. Genus

2. Variety

3. Class

4. Phylum/Division

5. Species

6. Order

7. Kingdom

8. Family

Anatomy of a flower

Can you correctly label the parts of the flower using the words below? For bonus points, which three of these labels make up the pistil and which two make up the stamen?

PLANT PARTS

- Ovary
- Peduncle
- Stigma
- Petal
- Filament
- Style
- Ovule
- Sepal
- Receptacle
- Anther

A.

B.

C.

G.

D.

E.

F.

H.

I.

J.

Answers: page 174

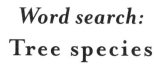
Word search:
Tree species

Listed below are the scientific names of several
well-known tree species. Can you find all of the
words given in capital letters in the grid? They may
be written in any direction, forwards or backwards,
including diagonally. For a bonus point, which of the
listed trees is pictured above?

WORDS TO SEARCH FOR

- Alder: *Alnus GLUTINOSA*
- Apple: *Malus DOMESTICA*
- Ash: *Fraxinus EXCELSIOR*
- Aspen: *Populus TREMULA*
- Cedar: *Cedrus LIBANI*
- Common beech:
  Fagus SYLVATICA
- Dogwood: *Cornus SANGUINEA*
- English oak: *Quercus ROBUR*
- Field elm: *Ulmus MINOR*
- Hazel: *Corylus AVELLANA*
- Holly: *Ilex AQUIFOLIUM*

- Monkey puzzle:
  Araucaria ARAUCANA
- Rowan: *Sorbus AUCUPARIA*
- Scots pine: *Pinus SYLVESTRIS*
- Silver birch: *Betula PENDULA*
- Sweet chestnut:
  Castanea SATIVA
- Walnut: *Juglans REGIA*
- White willow: *Salix ALBA*
- Wild cherry: *Prunus AVIUM*
- Yew: *Taxus BACCATA*

```
S A N G U I N E A U R C K A G
A U C U P A R I A P F R B H G
F R T B R E X C E L S I O R R
D O M E S T I C A M O N C U O
S A T I V A R O I O B U M B N
T L L K Q B E C A A M A U O I
R U J B R Q G C C U N G I R M
E D J Y A K I C I A L U L B Q
M N X N U T A V L U L E O A F
U E R N A T A L T T Z I F M J
L P L V A K E I I N A B I L I
A Q L D K V N H Q C A G U V Z
K Y Z F A O I V S B B T Q I R
S I R T S E V L Y S L H A I U
F X V A W L F A R A U C A N A
```

Anagrams: Structural terms

Rearrange the letters below to reveal eight
words relating to a plant's structure.

THE TERMS

1. NOTINERED
2. TAMOTAS
3. IDCAERL
4. UMULLEP
5. MYLEX
6. MOLEPH
7. IMESPIDER
8. LAPASIDE

Answers: page 174

All paired up

Draw horizontal and vertical lines to join each of these male and female flowers into pairs. Each pair must contain one red flower and one yellow flower. Lines cannot cross either one another or any flower. All flowers must be used in exactly one pair.

Multiple-choice: Botany brain busters

How many of these multiple-choice questions
do you know the answers to?

**1. Which of the plants pictured
below is *Helianthus annuus*?**

a) Wallflower

b) Moonflower

c) Sunflower

d) Starflower

2. What are angiosperms?

a) Flowering plants

b) Conifers

c) Ferns

d) Mosses

a.

b.

c.

d.

3. What type of plants are *Taxodium distichum* and *Metasequoia glyptostroboides*?

a) Deciduous conifers

b) Deep-water aquatic plants

c) Small-leaved alpines

d) Aromatic herbs

4. What type of tree holds the record for being the tallest in the world?

a) *Eucalyptus regnans*

b) *Sequoia sempervirens*

c) *Sequoiadendron giganteum*

d) *Pseudotsuga menziesii*

5. If a leaf is described as denticulate, what does this mean?

a) Downy surface on underside

b) Finely toothed

c) Deciduous

d) Grows near a fox's den

6. If a plant is said to have an 'indumentum' what characteristic is being described?

a) Bulbous stem

b) Cone-type seed

c) Single trunk

d) Covering of hair

7. What is the oak known as *Quercus suber* commercially used for?

a) Decking

b) Corks for wine bottles

c) Roof tiles

d) Beams/lintels in houses

8. Which one of the following is botanically classed as a berry?

a) Raspberry

b) Banana

c) Peach

d) Strawberry

9. What is *Sphagnum platyphyllum*?

a) Bamboo

b) Orchid

c) Moss

d) Fungal disease

10. Pictured below, *Hydrangea petiolaris* is what type of plant?

a) Climber

b) Tree

c) Upright shrub

d) Shrub that bears pinecones

Mix and match: Happy families

The plants listed below each belong to one of four families. Do you know which plant belongs where? Write the plant names or numbers below the correct family name, so that each group has four plants in total. Opposite are images of the plants to help you identify them.

THE PLANTS

1. *Cicer arietinum*
2. *Vanilla planifolia*
3. *Prunus armeniaca*
4. *Echinacea purpurea*
5. *Cydonia oblonga*
6. *Calendula officinalis*
7. *Tamarindus indica*
8. *Calypso bulbosa*
9. *Lotus corniculatus*
10. *Dactylorhiza viridis*
11. *Anthyllis vulneraria*
12. *Eriobotrya japonica*
13. *Cymbidium goeringii*
14. *Rubus chamaemorus*
15. *Taraxacum officinale*
16. *Achillea millefolium*

ROSACEAE	FABACEAE	ORCHIDACEAE	ASTERACEAE

1.

2.

3.

4.

5.

6.

7.

8.

9.

10.

11.

12.

13.

14.

15.

16.

Answers: page 175

Chapter Five
PLANT IDENTIFICATION

Tall trees or amazing annuals?

Size is not everything. Plants can be beautiful whether they are as tall as skyscrapers or only knee height. How well do you know your tall and mighty trees from those beautiful short-lived annuals? Below are the scientific names for six trees and six annuals. Can you place each one in the right group?

A. TREES

B. ANNUALS

SCIENTIFIC NAMES

1. *Papaver commutatum*
2. *Quercus robur*
3. *Sequoia sempervirens*
4. *Limnanthes douglasii*
5. *Liquidambar styraciflua*
6. *Helianthus annus*
7. *Lathyrus odoratus*
8. *Nothofagus dombeyi*
9. *Acer palmatum*
10. *Orlaya grandiflora*
11. *Nigella damascena*
12. *Nyssa sylvatica*

Answers: page 176

Dot to dot

Reveal a fruit by drawing straight lines to join the stars and dots in numerical order. Each time you reach a hollow star, lift your pen, and continue drawing from the next star. What is the fruit?

Answers: page 176

Match the leaf to the plant

How well do you know your variegated from your acicular? Try testing your leaf knowledge by matching these pictures of foliage with their scientific names.

A.

B.

C.

D.

E.

F.

PLANTS

1. *Liriodendron tulipifera*
2. *Monstera deliciosa*
3. *Jacobaea maritima*
4. *Fatsia japonica*
5. *Musa basjoo*
6. *Acanthus mollis*

6. *Dicksonia antartica*
8. *Acer palmatum*
9. *Vitis vinifera*
10. *Trachycarpus fortunei*
11. *Mimosa pudica*
12. *Cyclamen hederifolium*

G.

H.

I.

J.

K.

L.

Mix and match: Bulb, rhizome, corm or tuber?

Bulbs, rhizomes, corms and tubers are types of swollen underground roots that are used to store food and supply their plants with nutrients when needed. Looking at the list below, can you place each in one of the main groups? To help you out, there are three of each type.

THE PLANTS

1. Iris

2. Tulip

3. Gladiolus

4. Dahlia

5. Crocus

6. Canna lily

7. Ginger

8. Hyacinth

9. Potato

10. Cyclamen

11. Daffodil

12. Freesia

BULB

RHIZOME

CORM

TUBER

The germination game

Can you link each flower to its seed by drawing a series of paths, each connecting a flower and seed? No more than one path can enter any square, and paths can only travel horizontally or vertically between squares. The flowers and seeds are coloured so that you can be sure which flower results from which seed.

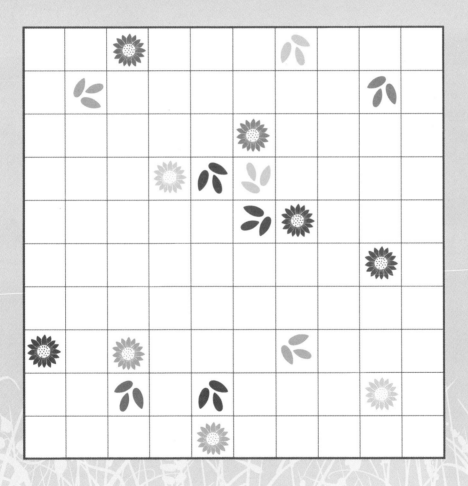

Mix and match: **Bulbtastic**

Match the genus with the species to reveal some of the most
beautiful bulbs in the world. To help you out, each of the bulbs is
pictured in full bloom, with a number corresponding to its genus.

GENUS

1. *Nerine*
2. *Scilla*
3. *Crocus*
4. *Narcissus*
5. *Galanthus*

6. *Anemone*
7. *Hyacinthus*
8. *Allium*
9. *Lilium*
10. *Tulipa*

SPECIES

A. *lancifolium*
B. *sphaerocephalon*
C. *bowdenii*
D. *blanda*
E. *nivalis*

F. *poeticus*
G. *orientalis*
H. *vernus*
I. *linifolia*
J. *siberica*

1.

2.

3.

4.

5.

6.

7.

8.

9.

10.

Answers: page 177

Deadly dozen

Which of the following plants are deadly and which are safe
to eat? For a bonus point, can you give the pictured plant its
scientific name from the list below?

THE PLANTS

1. *Digitalis purpurea*

2. *Brassica oleracea*

3. *Atropa belladonna*

4. *Allium porrum*

5. *Aconitum napellus*

6. *Ricinus communis*

7. *Raphanus sativus*

8. *Taxus bacatta*

9. *Beta vulgaris* subsp. *vulgaris*

10. *Conium maculatum*

11. *Lactuca sativa*

12. *Phaseolus coccineus*

Answers: page 177

Wordoku

Place A, C, D, E, L, M, O, R, S or T into each empty square in the wordoku, so that no letter repeats in any row, column or bold-lined 5 × 2 box. Once solved, the name of a family hinted at below the puzzle can be read down the shaded diagonal.

	M		R	T	D	E		C	
E			C			M			O
				O	E				
R	L							T	A
T		E					M		L
M		S					O		R
O	R							M	D
				S	R				
S			O			L			C
	T		M	A	O	S		D	

- Chamomile
- Dahlia
- Daisy
- Gerbera
- Sunflower
- Zinnia

Coming up roses

Growing in a range of stunning colours, many with scent that fills the air, roses are among the most popular garden shrubs. Can you group the following varieties by colour? Each group has a total of four rose varieties. To help you out, each of the flowers is pictured on the opposite page but not in the right order.

THE VARIETIES

1. 'Iceberg'
2. 'Wilhelm'
3. 'Arthur Bell'
4. 'Canary Bird'
5. 'Trumpeter'
6. 'Alba'
7. 'Desdemona'
8. 'Darcey Bussell'
9. 'Graham Thomas'
10. 'Crimson Shower'
11. 'Claire Austin'
12. 'Charlotte'

WHITE/CREAM

RED

YELLOW

A.

B.

C.

D.

E.

F.

G.

H.

I.

J.

K.

L.

Answers: page 178

Anagrams: Mustard mayhem

The plants listed below all belong to the *Brassicaceae* family, sometimes known as the mustard family. But their letters have all been jumbled up. Can you unscramble the letters to reveal the names of these popular edible food crops?

1. BEBAGAC
2. REFLOWUCLIA
3. LAKE
4. CIBROCOL
5. RHLOABIK
6. PIRUNT
7. SHIRAD
8. KRETOC
9. ASE ALEK
10. SABIWA

Buried berries

This puzzle works like a minesweeper, but instead of mines, you are looking for poisonous berries! The numbers in some of the squares reveal the total count of berries in touching squares – including diagonally. No more than one berry may be placed per square, and they cannot be hiding in numbered squares.

	1			2		
2		2		2		2
				1	2	
2	3	1	2			2
			2		3	2
3				2		
	4		3		2	1

Answers: page 178

Chapter Six

GARDENING TECHNIQUES

Which technique?

Harry the horticulturist has been asked to undertake a 'whip and tongue' on his apple tree. Which of the images below illustrates what he should be doing? How many of the other techniques can you identify?

TECHNIQUES

1. Whip and tongue
2. Chip bud
3. Layering a shoot

4. Collecting seed
5. Potting on a plant
6. Pricking out

A.

B.

C.

D.

E.

F.

Answers: page 179

Field work

Draw along the dashed lines to split this field into 11 allotments, so that each allotment contains exactly one watering can. Every allotment must be a square, measuring 1×1 units or larger, and there must be no unused areas left over.

Word search: **Peat-free compost**

Listed here are 10 ingredients you might find in your peat-free compost mix when potting up your plants. Can you find them in the word search below?

```
I  K  Q  X  P  B  B  L  H  L  V  E  B  Z  F  Q  T  H  Q  L
V  W  W  E  L  V  A  T  O  F  C  I  W  J  W  B  S  N  P  Y
D  Q  G  X  K  P  G  A  R  F  R  H  Q  U  A  L  Y  C  C  Y
M  A  K  Z  A  B  L  K  T  Q  F  J  E  G  U  L  I  Y  J  J
I  B  Q  P  U  Z  J  F  I  X  C  N  T  N  C  O  W  Q  L  Y
X  M  O  R  O  F  M  V  C  I  O  U  O  W  P  O  F  A  F  E
S  W  L  E  E  G  A  O  U  B  C  P  Y  O  E  W  Q  M  I  L
Y  O  Z  R  T  Y  P  D  L  U  O  I  B  O  R  E  Q  Y  L  M
T  W  Z  B  I  O  N  U  T  I  N  K  U  D  L  N  D  F  N  G
O  Q  M  I  L  B  C  P  U  K  U  W  N  C  I  O  H  K  K  K
H  Y  S  F  U  Q  Q  W  R  S  T  A  K  H  T  T  A  V  B  F
E  M  W  D  C  R  D  T  A  B  F  V  N  I  E  S  V  T  Z  Z
Y  W  A  O  I  J  F  W  L  L  I  S  G  P  W  D  H  S  M  U
I  T  G  O  M  O  J  K  G  U  B  K  H  P  S  R  M  U  N  L
A  H  O  W  R  U  Y  H  R  N  R  B  T  I  V  D  B  D  D  D
Q  W  D  Q  E  U  M  U  I  L  E  R  B  N  Y  K  N  W  N  X
J  H  I  H  V  V  Y  M  T  I  G  I  L  G  E  D  N  A  S  M
F  C  L  F  X  S  K  V  Z  J  D  Q  K  S  K  D  J  S  Y  U
Q  O  E  O  K  D  G  O  V  H  J  O  J  C  Z  N  I  N  S  T
C  N  F  Y  B  F  Z  U  V  L  O  O  W  K  C  O  R  P  K  L
```

INGREDIENTS

- Sand
- Vermiculite
- Perlite
- Horticultural grit
- Wood chippings
- Coconut fibre
- Woodfibre
- Rockwool
- Stonewool
- Sawdust

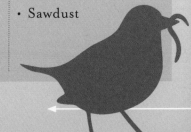

Lawn loop

Imagine you are about to walk in a loop around your lawn
wearing a pair of spiked sandals in order to help aerate your
garden turf. Draw a loop that visits every white square, but
without visiting any square more than once to avoid over aeration.
The loop must be made up only of horizontal and vertical lines,
and cannot enter any black squares.

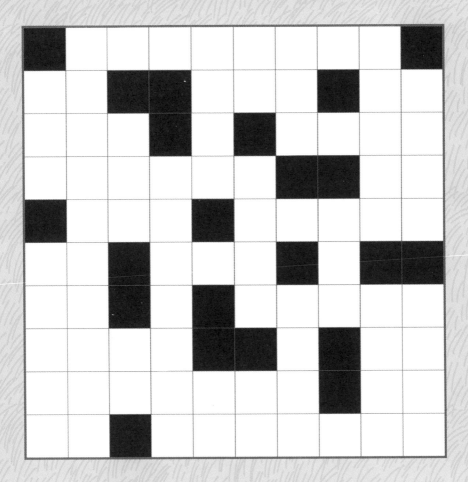

Hanjie: Shading by numbers

Reveal a fruit crop in the grid by shading some squares according to the given clue numbers. The clues provide, in reading order from left to right or top to bottom, the length of every run of consecutive shaded squares in each row and column. There must be a gap of at least one empty square between each run of shaded squares in the same row or column. For further help in solving the puzzle, turn to page 24.

PICTURE HINTS

1. This fruit's parent plant is the *Solanum lycopersicum*.

2. The plant responds particularly well to the pinching out of laterals.

3. Best-known varieties are red, but they can also be yellow, purple or black.

4. The juice of this fruit is the national drink of the US state of Ohio.

5. The fruit's name ends with the same two letters as it begins – fill in the blanks below the puzzle.

Column clues (top):

```
                                    I
                                  2   2
        I                     I   2  2  2  I
      2  3  2              2  2  4  I  2  2  I  3
   3  5  2  2              2  2  5  3  4  2  2  4
   3  2  2  5  5  5  3  2  2  5  3  4  2  2  4
   3  2  5  3  8  I  9  2  5  I  2  3  4  5  6
```

Row clues (left):

- 3, 2, 2, I
- 2, 3, I
- I, 3, 3
- 5, 3
- I, 3, 3, I
- 5, 2, 2
- 3, 2, 2
- 2, 3, I
- 3, I, 5
- 5, I, 2, 2
- 2, 2, I, 3
- 5, I
- 9
- I, 5
- I, I, 3, I
- 2, I, 5, 2
- 5, 3, 3
- I, 2, 4
- 4, 5
- 2, 6

Name of fruit: _ _ M _ T _

Answers: page 180

Compost conundrum: Green or brown?

Gary the gardener has turned up at work to discover that the compost is slimy. The head gardener tells him there is too much nitrogen-based (green) material in the compost heap and instructs him to add more carbon-based (brown) material. Of the 12 materials listed below, circle the four best materials that Gary should choose.

1. ONIONS

2. DOG FAECES

3. FRUIT SCRAPS

4. FISH SCRAPS

5. GRATED CHEESE

6. FALLEN LEAVES

7. GRASS CLIPPINGS

8. SHREDDED PAPER

9. WOOD CHIPPINGS

10. VEGETABLE SCRAPS

11. HERBACEOUS CLIPPINGS

12. SHREDDED CARDBOARD BOXES

Fences

Finish adding twine between this grid of posts in order to mark out a set of straight lines for planting seeds. The twine must be placed so it forms a single loop, without crossing or touching itself at any point. Only horizontal and vertical lines between the posts are allowed. Some pieces of twine are already given, and cannot be moved.

The cutting edge

There are many different ways to train a tree or a shrub so that it takes on a particular shape. Ten different shapes are listed below. Fill in the gaps to reveal what they are.

1. _ S P _ _ _ _ R
2. F _ _ _ HE _ _ _ / T _ _ _
3. _ A I _ _ _ / _ _ P
4. _ _ _ _ QU _ / C _ _ D _ _
5. _ PR _ _ _ _ / _ _ R _ _ N
6. _ T _ _ _ _ RD
7. M _ _ T _ - S _ _ _ _ D/ _ _ EE
8. _ P _ _ - _ _ _ RE / _ _ B _ _ T
9. _ L _ _ CH _ _
10. _ _ N

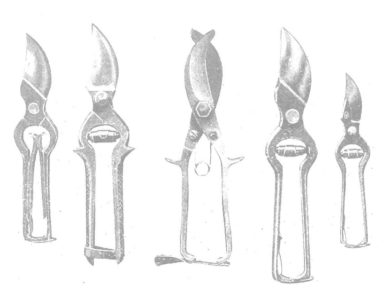

Anagrams: Techniques with a twist

Below are some activities that you might find yourself doing in the garden, but their letters have been scrambled. Can you rearrange the letters to put the 'ing' into gardening?

1. NUPR *ING*

2. GDGI *ING*

3. CHULM *ING*

4. TASK *ING*

5. NLATP *ING*

6. DEWE *ING*

7. OHE *ING*

8. KAR *ING*

9. WOM *ING*

10. WOS *ING*

Answers: page 181

Yearly rotation

Imagine you have 16 raised beds for growing different vegetables and want to rotate the crops so that no crop is planted in the same bed twice in 16 years. Number the squares in the grid so that each square contains a number from 1 to 16. Each number must appear exactly once and should be in a square that points in the precise direction of the next highest number (although it may not necessarily be in an immediately neighbouring square).

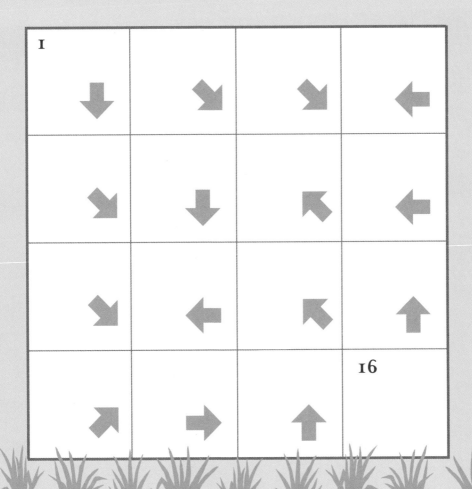

Mix and match: The green grass of home

A tip-top lawn requires plenty of care and attention. Pictured opposite are some of the tools you might use to keep you grass looking its best. Can you identify each tool from the list below?

TOOLS

1. Half moon
2. Strimmer
3. Cylinder mower
4. Rotary mower
5. Edging shears
6. Aerator spikes
7. Weeding tool
8. Turfing iron
9. Spreader
10. Roller
11. Leaf rake
12. Scarifier machine

A.

B.

C.

D.

E.

F.

G.

H.

I.

J.

K.

L.

Answers: page 181

Multiple-choice: Gardening techniques

Test your gardening knowledge by answering the following
multiple-choice questions.

**1. What would you use to prune
the young shoots on a rosebush?**

a) Secateurs

b) True lute

c) Bow saw

d) Hack saw

**2. What causes the stripes to
appear on a lawn?**

a) The type of grass used

b) A roller on the back of a mower

c) The time of day it is mown

d) By scarifying the lawn first

**3. What is the technique used
for laying organic material on
the surface of soil instead of
digging it?**

a) Avoid dig

b) No dig

c) Dig you not

d) Bad big

**4. What are the unwanted
shoots called that sometimes
appear at the base of a tree
or shrub?**

a) Gullible

b) Trick

c) Sucker

d) Liar

5. What are loppers used for?

a) Making holes in the ground

b) Supporting heavy limbs

c) Levelling out a lawn

d) Cutting branches

6. What's the name of the propagation technique whereby a stem is put in contact with the soil when still attached to the main plant?

a) Layering

b) Briaring

c) Smoothing

d) Contacting

7. What is the technique called whereby groups of plants are placed close to each other for mutual benefits?

a) Companion planting

b) Friendship planting

c) Company planting

d) Buddy planting

8. Name the Japanese technique of pruning branches on a tree into clusters of shapes.

a) Fog pruning

b) Cloud pruning

c) Float pruning

d) Drift pruning

9. Which of the following is not considered a benefit of using mulch?

a) Keeping the soil warm

b) Drying out damp soil

c) Keeping the soil moist

d) Preventing weeds

10. Which of the following terms could be used to describe plants grown in partial light?

a) Artificial photosynthesis

b) Aquaponics

c) Hydroponics

d) Etiolation

Answers: page 181

Chapter Seven
GARDENS AROUND THE WORLD

Mix and match: Location finder

Link each of the following clues to a world-famous botanical
garden. Three are pictured opposite – do you know which?

1. This botanical garden has a public
exhibition space that is also home to
the largest living interior green wall
in the southern hemisphere.

2. These gardens are famous for their
rock garden featuring 15 stones of
different sizes set in groups and
surrounded by white gravel.

3. In which botanical garden can
you visit the Orquidário, home to
600 species of orchids and Pedro
Cachimbo rose garden?

4. Epitomizing the principles of
Renaissance design and aesthetics,
this garden was considered hugely
influential on the development of
garden design throughout Europe.

5. This botanical garden lies on the
eastern slopes of Table Mountain,
on land once owned by Cecil Rhodes.

6. In which of the botanical gardens
will you find a Cubist villa that
currently houses a museum?

LOCATIONS

A. Kirstenbosch, Cape Town

B. Majorelle Garden, Marrakech

C. Jardim Botânico, Rio de Janeiro

D. Royal Botanic Gardens of Sydney

E. Villa d'Este Gardens, Tivoli

F. Ryoan-ji, Kyoto

Answers: page 182

Palatial spaces

Listed below are eight famous garden palaces from around the world, but some of their letters are missing. We have given the name of the palace and the country in which it can be found. Can you fill in the blanks?

1. Name of Palace: P E _ E _ H _ F
   Country: _ U _ _ _ A

2. Name of Palace: A L _ _ M _ R _
   Country: S _ _ I _

3. Name of Palace: _ R O _ T N _ _ G H _ _ M
   Country: _ W E _ _ _

4. Name of Palace: H _ _ P T _ _ / _ O U _ _
   Country: E _ _ L _ _ D

5. Name of Palace: C _ _ T _ _ / G A _ _ O L _ O
   Country: _ T A _ Y

6. Name of Palace: S A _ _ S _ _ C _
   Country: _ E R _ _ N _

7. Name of Palace: M _ G _ _ L / G A _ _ _ N
   Country: I _ _ _ A

8. Name of Palace: R O _ A _ / G _ _ _ N H _ U _ E S / _ F / L _ _ K _ N
   Country: B _ L _ _ U M

Triangle conundrum

Copy the letters from each of the loose triangular pieces onto an empty triangle in the grid, so that each row of letters spells out the name of a 'Capability' Brown garden. None of the triangles should be rotated.

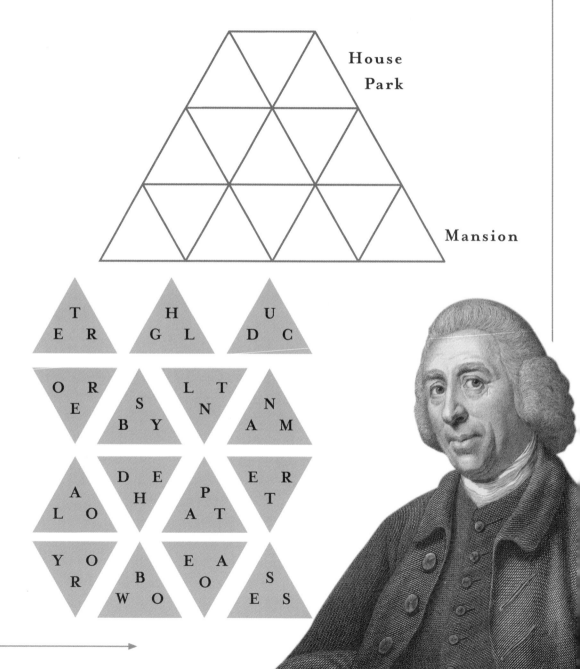

House
Park

Mansion

Where am I?

Can you guess which world-famous garden I am from the clues below? Score 12 points if you solve the puzzle with one clue and deduct a point for every additional clue that you need.

1. Pictured opposite, my gardens cover 32 hectares (79 acres) of land, and I am considered to be the largest 'flower' garden in the world.

2. I opened to visitors in 1949 to showcase my famous flower displays.

3. My grounds also include a Japanese garden, an English landscape garden, a spring meadow and a garden maze.

4. I was created in 1857, as an English landscape garden.

5. My name means 'kitchen garden', but I am not famous for either fruit or vegetables.

6. I am often referred to as the Garden of Europe.

7. I only open to visitors for eight weeks of the year, yet I attract almost 800,000 visitors in that time.

8. Seven million bulbs are planted each year in my garden and they are all supplied for free by 100 bulb growers.

9. My gardens are just outside of Lisse in the Netherlands.

10. I am world famous for bulbs, particularly tulips.

Answers: page 182

Spot the difference

Squashes and watermelons can look quite similar on the vine, but
can you spot five differences between the two images below?

Answers: page 183

Garden maze

Prepare for tackling your next garden maze, such as the famous hedge maze at Hampton Court, by solving the following puzzle. Enter at the top and then exit at the bottom while taking as few wrong turns as you can.

VERSAILLES

ENTRIES TO FIND

- ANDRE LE NOTRE
- BAROQUE
- BASSIN D'APOLLON
- BASSIN DE LATONE
- CHATEAU
- CLAUDE MOLLET
- COLONNADE
- DU BUS
- FOUNTAINS
- FRANCE
- GRAND CANAL
- GROTTE DE THETYS
- HILAIRE MASSON
- LAWNS
- LOUIS
- ORANGERY
- PALACE
- PARTERRES
- SUN KING
- TRIANON

Gardens of Versailles

Find the listed entries written in the grid in
any direction, including diagonally. They may also
be written backwards. Which features from this list
can be seen in the picture on the opposite page?

```
G T E L L O M E D U A L C B U
M R N N P A L A C E Y E A D A
A U O S E S A S T R G S A N S
A A S T S D N U E R S L D I U
P E S R T W A G A I U R U R N
A T A U A E N N I E O A A K
R A M L S A D D N L L E L N I
T H E E R C A E E O U C R O N
E C R O A P E N T Q L D I N G
R A I N O N O C O H P O T A S
R E A L E T S R N S E T C I U
E L L S R G A S E A I T T R B
S O I E O B E T T E R O Y T U
N T H S N I A T N U O F S S D
N E N O T A L E D N I S S A B
```

City park identifier

How many of the city parks and gardens can you identify
from these photographs? Their cities are listed, but
not in the correct order. To help you out, you'll find
a clue in brackets for each city name. Like a crossword clue,
it tells you how many words are in the name and how many
letters in each word.

A.

B.

C.

D.

PARKS AND GARDENS

1. New York, USA (7, 4)
2. Berlin, Germany (10)
3. Paris, France (6, 2, 10)
4. Bangkok, Thailand (7, 4)

5. London, UK (4, 4)
6. Vancouver, Canada (7, 4)
7. Madrid, Spain (2, 6)
8. Copenhagen, Denmark (6, 7)

E.

F.

G.

H.

Answers: page 184

Anagrams: Garden styles through time

There have been many styles of gardening through the ages.
Unscramble the letters below to reveal 10 historic horticultural
periods or styles. One is pictured opposite as a clue.

1. QUEDEGARNES

2. SCETUQUEPIR

3. CHEFRN QUEAROB

4. ZANYNIBET

5. ENISTICHELL

6. NEPSRIA

7. DESTIMORN

8. STICRATUALIN

9. SOAMIANPOTME

10. GLINESH SCALANDPE MENTVEMO

Answers: page 184

Word fit: **World gardens**

Can you place the capitalized names in the list of famous gardens into the grid? Write one letter per grid square so that each capitalized entry can be read either across or down, crossword style. For extra points, can you identify the four gardens on the opposite page? They all feature in the puzzle.

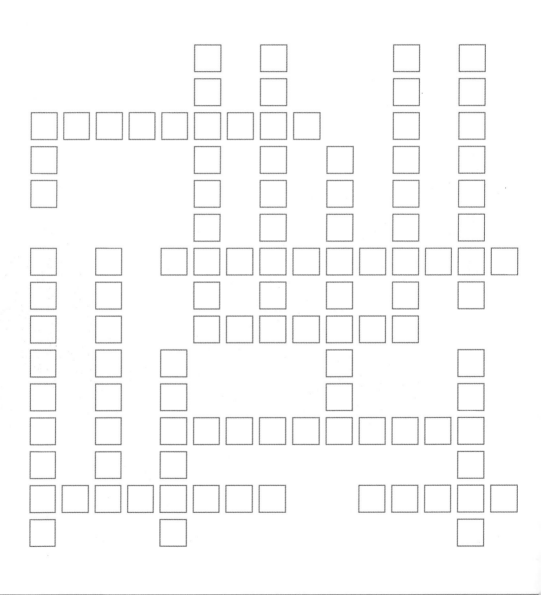

FAMOUS GARDENS

- BROOKLYN [Botanic Garden]
- [Chateau de] VERSAILLES
- HIDCOTE
- HIGHGROVE
- KEUKENHOF
- KEW [Gardens]
- [Le Jardin] MAJORELLE
- [Les Jardins de Claude] MONET
- LONGLEAT
- NONG NOOCH [Tropical Botanical Garden]
- POWERSCOURT [Gardens]
- [Schloss] SANSSOUCI
- STOURHEAD [Gardens]
- The BUTCHART [Gardens]
- [Villa D'Este], TIVOLI
- WISLEY

A.

B.

C.

D.

Answers: page 184

Chapter Eight

GARDEN FEATURES AND DESIGN

Anagrams: Muddled methods

Rearrange the letters in the words below to reveal eight
different approaches to gardening.

1. MIDILETTER HOTDEM

2. MYCODIBAIN

3. TURULECAMPER

4. PHONYOSCRID

5. COIRANG

6. QUAINSCOPA

7. ON GID

8. MOCOPANIN

Answers: page 185

Up the garden path

Design a path that visits every empty square in this garden,
without visiting any square more than once. You must make a
continuous loop using only horizontal and vertical lines,
and cannot enter any of the black squares.

Sustainable gardening

Can you identify the gardening practices pictured below? To help you out, some of the letters have been filled in already.

1. H _ G _ _ _ U _ _ _ R
2. _ A _ S E _ / _ E _
3. _ T _ _ W / _ _ L _
4. C _ _ T _ _ N _ _
5. _ Q _ _ R _ F _ _ _
6. L _ _ _ G _ _

1.

2.

3.

4.

5.

6.

Answers: page 185

Building bridges

Below are lots of little islands in a water garden. Can you add
horizontal or vertical lines to make bridges between them?

In the finished layout each island must
connect to at least one other island and all the
islands form a single network. Each island has
a number. This tells you how many bridges are
connected to it in total. There can never be
more than two bridges between the same pair
of islands and no bridges may cross.

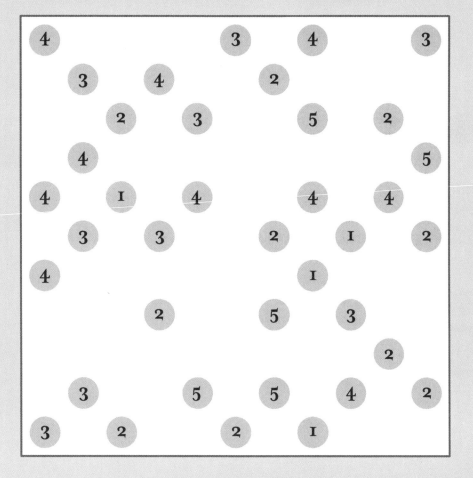

Multiple-choice: Garden features

How good is your knowledge of garden features?
Find out with this multiple-choice quiz.

1. What name is given to a formal planting area, usually outside a grand house, in which the flower beds are displayed in intricate shapes?

a) Parterre

b) Marterre

c) Sonterre

d) Granterre

2. Which of the following terms describes a hidden ditch that is used to keep livestock out of the garden?

a) Tee hee

b) Ha ha

c) LOL

d) Ho-ho

3. A garden structure that is not actually a proper building, but just pretending to be, is known as a . . .?

a) Mistake

b) Glitch

c) Trickery

d) Folly

4. What is the name for a formal garden that often contain herbs and is bordered by low-growing formal hedges?

a) Knot garden

b) Bowline garden

c) Reef garden

d) Ribbon garden

5. An attractive garden structure in which doves are kept is known as a . . .?

a) Dovecrib

b) Dovecote

c) Dovepillow

d) Dovebed

6. Which of the following terms is used to describe an ornate area of garden allocated for fruit, vegetables and herbs?

a) Panager

b) Mugager

c) Cupager

d) Potager

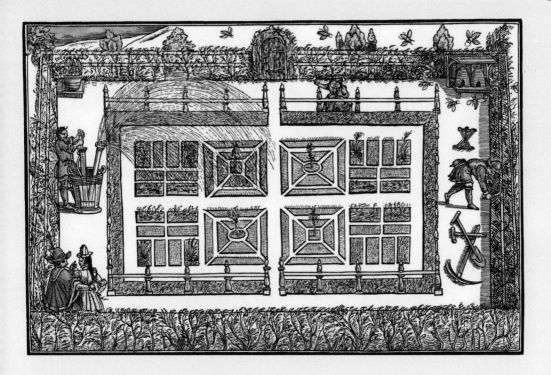

7. What is a *roji* in a Japanese garden?

a) A dewy path

b) An ornate red bridge

c) A seat made of moss

d) A contrast of foliage between Japanese maples

8. Which of the following terms describes an area of woodland that is used for growing plant supports and climbing structures by cutting trees and shrubs low to the ground every few years?

a) Coppice

b) Twiglet

c) Stumpery

d) Meadery

9) What is the name for an elaborately decorated natural or artificial cave that was a popular garden feature in 18th-century Europe?

a) Dirtto

b) Mudatto

c) Grotto

d) Growetto

10) Which of the following terms describes a walkway that is usually bordered with neatly clipped trees or hedges?

a) Allée

b) Piedmapants

c) Camberelle

d) Tracker

Answers: page 186

Sunshine or shade?

Listed below are five plants that prefer heavy shade and five that favour bright sunshine. Which plants would you place in the sunny side of the border, and which would you put in the deepest shade? For a bonus point, which of the listed plants is pictured?

THE PLANTS

1. *Lavandula angustifolia*
2. *Hedera helix*
3. *Iris foetidissima*
4. *Eranthis hyemalis*
5. *Anemone nemorosa*

6. *Sanvitalia procumbens*
7. *Echinops ritro*
8. *Brunnera macrophylla*
9. *Citrus × aurantiifolia*
10. *Lantana camara*

DEEPEST SHADE

FULL SUN

Answers: page 186

Garden folly

You are designing a garden with several follies, each to be accompanied by a bench. Place a bench next to each folly, so that every row and column contains the given number of benches as shown by the clues outside the grid. Benches can only be placed in one of the up to four empty squares immediately above, below or to the side of a folly. No two benches can touch, however – not even diagonally.

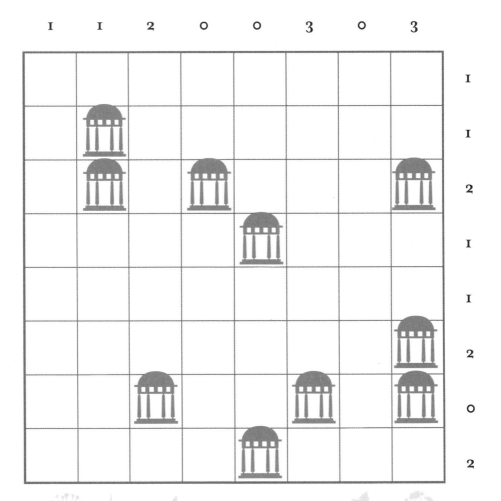

Garden installations

Here are 10 features commonly found in a garden. Do you know what they are? The name of each is given, but can you fill in the gaps?

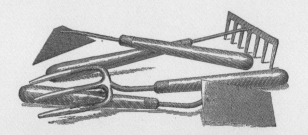

1. _ A R _ E _ U _

2. _ E _ K _ _ G

3. _ A E _ / _ E T _ R _

4. _ A _ _ O

5. _ EA _ IN _ / _ R A

6. _ E _ _ A _ E

7. _ OR _ E _ Y

8. _ A _ ER / _ UT _

9. _ OM _ O _ T / _ E _ P

10. _ OL _ / _ RA _ E _

Answers: page 186

Mix and match: Garden planting

Each of the plants listed below favours a specific location in a
garden. See if you can place each one in its rightful home.

PLANTS

A. *Delphinium elatum*
B. *Athyrium filix-femina*
C. *Malus domestica*
D. *Lactuca sativa*
E. *Pinus sylvestris*
F. *Nelumbo nucifera*
G. *Citrus × paradisi*
H. *Lewisia longipetala*

GARDEN LOCATIONS

1. Fernery

2. Alpine bed

3. Fruit garden

4. Water feature in conservatory

5. Pinetum

6. Herbaceous border

7. Orangery

8. Vegetable bed

Answers: page 187

Spot the difference

Here is a challenging garden plan. Can you spot five
differences between the two versions?

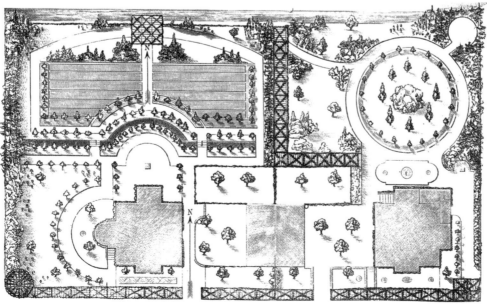

Past masters

Listed below are the names of 15 famous landscape architects and garden designers. Can you match the people up with the years they lived? For extra points, can you identify the three people pictured below?

THE LANDSCAPE GARDENERS

1. Corajoud Michel
2. Herta Hammerbacher
3. André Le Nôtre
4. Thomas Church
5. Frederick Law Olmsted
6. John Brookes
7. Gertrude Jekyll

8. Norah Lindsay
9. John Tradescant the younger
10. Geoffrey Jellicoe
11. Pechère René
12. Roberto Burle Marx
13. Vita Sackville-West
14. Brenda Colvin
15. Peter Joseph Lenné

A.

B.

C.

TIMELINE

1608–62

....

1613–1700

....

1789–1866

....

1822–1903

....

1843–1932

....

1866–1948

....

1892–1962

....

1897–1981

....

1900–85

....

1900–96

....

1902–78

....

1908–2002

....

1909–94

....

1937–2014

....

1933–2018

....

Answers: page 187

Chapter Nine

TALES FROM THE POTTING SHED

Tools to test you

They might be easy to identify when looking at them in the tool shed, but can you figure out what they are when written down with some of the letters missing? See if you can work out what these popular garden tools are.

1. A pointed tool used to make holes in the soil or compost for seed

_ _ B B _ R

2. A heated box used to encourage seeds to germinate

_ R _ P _ G _ T _ _

3. A pair of long-handled cutters

_ OP _ _ R _

4. Used to cut the blades of grass at the edge of the lawn

_ _ G _ _ G _ H _ A _ _

5. Sharp hand tool used for pruning

_ _ C _ T _ U _ _

6. Used for turning over the soil

_ _ T _ V _ T _ _

7. Used to push gardening materials around the garden

_ H _ E _ _ A _ RO _

8. A type of rake used for scarifying the lawn

_ P _ _ _ G _ I _ E _ A _ E

9. A large type of lawnmower

_ I _ E _ N

10. Can be used to water the garden with

_ AT _ _ _ _ _ _ A _

11. A short-handled weeding
implement
_ N _ _ N _ O _

12. An implement used for
removing weeds from a lawn
_ AI _ Y _ R _ B _ E _

Answers: page 188

Planting out

Sally the gardener has been given a list of plants, but she isn't sure which area of the garden to plant them in. Can you help her sort the plants into their most appropriate areas by listing their numbers in the right boxes – there are six in each group. For extra points, which plant in each group is pictured?

THE PLANTS

1. *Amelanchier lamarckii*
2. *Cupressocyparis leylandii*
3. *Nyssa sylvatica*
4. *Asplenium scolopendrium*
5. *Echinops ritro*
6. *Abies koreana*
7. *Athyrium niponicum*
8. *Hippuris vulgaris*
9. *Callitriche stagnalis*
10. *Thuja plicata*

11. *Dryopteris filix-mas*
12. *Osmunda regalis*
13. *Chamaecyparis lawsoniana*
14. *Matteuccia struthiopteris*
15. *Dicksonia antarctica*
16. *Sedum spectabile*
17. *Cryptomeria japonica*
18. *Hottonia palustris*
19. *Echinacea purpurea*
20. *Quercus rubra*

21. *Verbena bonariensis*
22. *Alchemilla mollis*
23. *Hydrocharis morsus-ranae*
24. *Taxus baccata*
25. *Hemerocallis fulva*
26. *Ranunculus hederaceus*
27. *Acer palmatum*
28. *Cercidiphyllum japonicum*
29. *Liquidambar styraciflua*
30. *Nymphaea alba*

FERNERY

CONIFER GLADE

HERBACEOUS PERENNIAL BORDER

DECIDUOUS TREES FOR AUTUMN COLOUR

IN THE POND (AQUATIC PLANTS)

Answers: page 188

Spot the difference

Here is a pretty jumble of plants. Can you spot the five differences
between the top and bottom images?

Perfect lawn wordoku

Reveal a tool that might be used to help prepare a lawn by placing A, C, E, F, I, L, R, S or T into each empty square, so that no letter repeats in any row, column or bold-lined 3 × 3 box. Once solved, the name of the tool can be read down the shaded diagonal.

		I	F			L	A	
		T		A		E		
L	R		T		C		I	F
I		C				F		E
	A						C	
E		R				T		I
C	F		E		R		S	A
		S		F		L		
		E	I		S	C		

Beans

Attach exactly one beanpole to each bean, so that every row and column contains the given number of poles. Beanpoles can only be placed in one of the up to four empty squares immediately above, below or to the side of a bean. No two beanpoles can touch – not even diagonally.

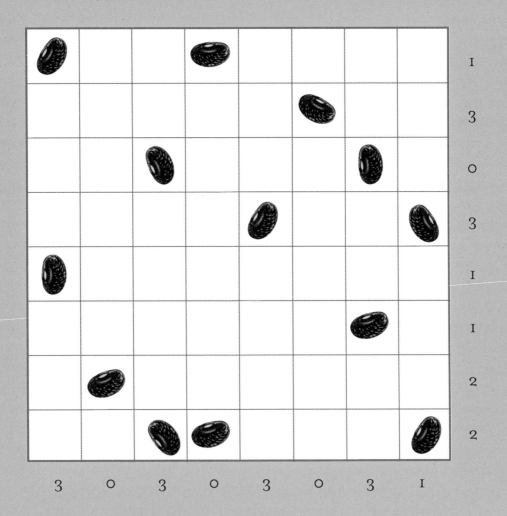

Anagrams: Potting shed staples

Unscramble the following words to reveal eight things
you might find in the potting shed.

1. GRINST

2. EDES TAPSECK

3. WOLFSTOPER

4. WELTOR

5. EATUCRESS

6. ERILIFTERZ

7. REGINTAW NAC

8. TOPGINT BLEAT

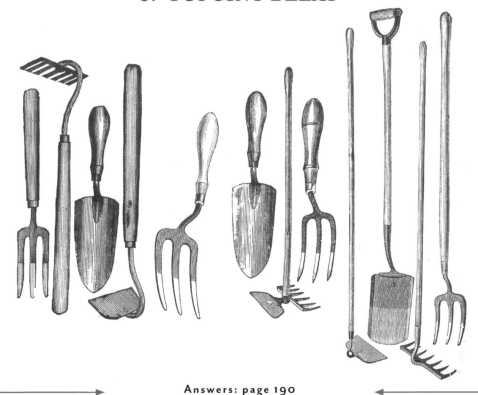

Answers: page 190

Wheelbarrow path

Imagine you've raked your lawn, making 16 neat piles of leaves for
composting. You now want to collect the leaves, visiting each pile
in turn and following the easiest route for your wheelbarrow
based on its increasing weight.

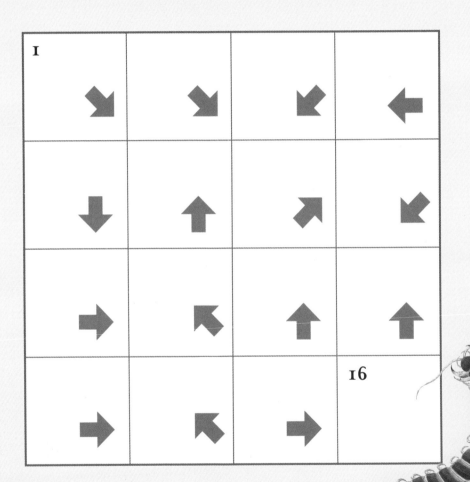

To work out your route, add numbers to the grid so
that each square contains a number from 1 to 16, with
no repeats. Every number must be in a square that
points in the precise direction of the next highest
number (although that number may not necessarily
be in an immediately neighbouring square).

Answers: page 190

Propagation methods

Gardeners use lots of different methods to propagate plants. Can you match the techniques in the pictures with the descriptions below?

THE METHODS

1. DIVISION
2. PRICKING OUT
3. HARDWOOD CUTTING
4. DIRECT SOWING
5. BUDDING
6. LEAF CUTTING
7. HEEL CUTTING
8. OFFSET PROPAGATION

A.

B.

C.

D.

E.

F.

G.

H.

Answers: page 190

What am I?

Can you guess what I am from the clues below, using the correct traditional name for me? Score 10 points if you solve the puzzle with one clue and deduct a point for every additional clue that you need.

I. There are five letters in my name.

2. I'm often used in lawn care as well as other aspects of gardening.

3. You might also see me used in traditional housework.

4. In fact, I have been used for work inside and outside houses for thousands of years.

5. My last letter is a M.

6. I can easily be made from a bundle of sticks and a stout handle.

7. My name begins with B.

8. In folklore, I am often used for witches to fly around on.

9. No, I am not a broom . . . or a brush although those can be used as alternative names for me.

Tilling the soil

Imagine you are using a rotavator to till the soil in your as-yet-unplanted allotment, and want to mark out a route using only straight lines that will cover the whole plot. Plan out a route that forms a single loop, without crossing or touching itself at any point. Only horizontal and vertical lines between the dots are allowed. Some lines have already been tilled, and cannot be moved.

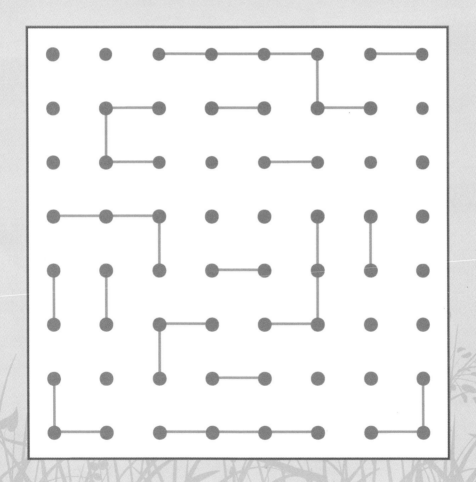

Mix and match: Fit for the task

Match each garden implement to
the task it is required to do.

THE TASKS

1. Pruning a hedge
2. Weeding
3. Cutting long grass

4. Creating a straight line to mark a border
5. Loosening the surface of the soil
6. Cutting a branch

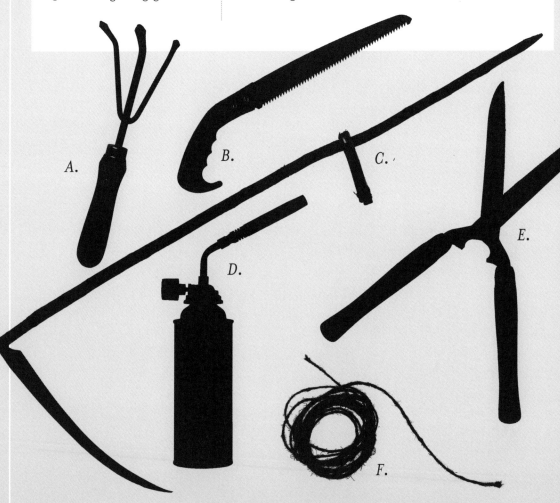

A.

B.

C.

D.

E.

F.

Dot to dot

Reveal a pair of essential tools by drawing straight lines to
join the stars and dots in increasing numerical order.

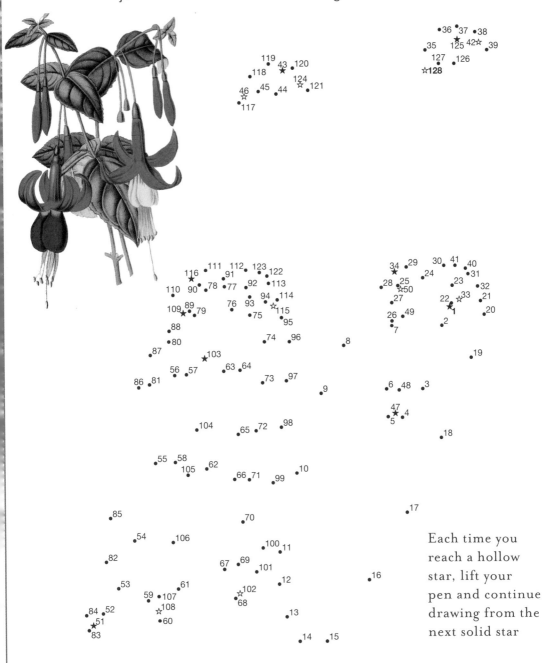

Each time you
reach a hollow
star, lift your
pen and continue
drawing from the
next solid star

ANSWERS

Answers
Chapter One: Kitchen Gardening

Puzzle 1: *What am I?*

I am a peach.

Puzzle 2: *Four but no more!*

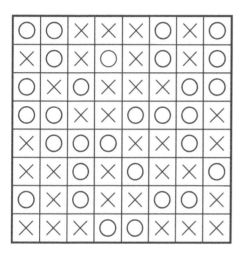

Puzzle 3: *Fruit-filled still lifes*

1. *Still Life with Lemons, ORANGES and a Rose* by Francisco de Zurbarán
2. *Jar of PEACHES* by Claude Monet
3. *The Meal*, also known as *The BANANAS* by Paul Gauguin
4. *Basket of APPLES* by Paul Cézanne
5. *POMEGRANATES* by John Singer Sargent
6. *Still Life with Apples, Pears, LEMONS and Grapes* by Vincent Van Gogh

Puzzle 4: *Planting seeds*

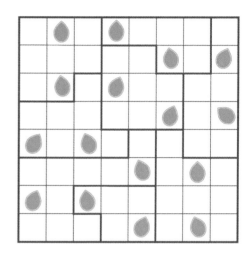

Puzzle 5: *Gourmet variety*

1. Plum; photo B
2. Apple; photo A
3. Tomato; photo F
4. Potato; photo G
5. Carrot; photo I
6. Parsnip; photo L
7. Beetroot; photo D
8. Runner bean; photo E
9. Pea; photo C
10. Lettuce; photo H
11. Rhubarb; photo J
12. Brussel sprout; photo K

Puzzle 6: Anagrams: *Mixed salad*

1. PARSNIP
2. KOHLRABI
3. BRUSSEL SPROUT
4. CARROT
5. CHERRY
6. GUAVA
7. MINT
8. FENNEL
9. CHILLI
10. POTATO
11. ROSEMARY
12. BEETROOT
13. THYME
14. BANANA
15. ORANGE

Puzzle 7: *Edible parts*

A. **Leaf:** Kale, spinach, cabbage, rocket, lettuce
B. **Root/Tuber:** Potato, carrot, sweet potato, beetroot, parsnip
C. **Flower:** Artichoke, cauliflower, borage, broccoli, nasturtium

Puzzle 8: *Shapely edibles*

1. Kohlrabi; photo A
2. Celeriac; photo J
3. Okra; photo I
4. Amaranthus; photo E
5. Cardoon; photo K
6. Seakale; photo B
7. Asparagus; photo L
8. Broad bean; photo H
9. Sweet potato; photo G
10. Lemongrass; photo D
11. Luffa; photo F
12. Black salsify; photo C

Puzzle 9: Quick quiz: *Know your onions*

1. Potato
2. Parsley
3. Tomato
4. Rhubarb
5. Gooseberry
6. Fig wasp
7. Dark green
8. Grape vine
9. Beetroot
10. Cauliflower and broccoli
11. Tarragon
12. Chilli

Puzzle 10: *Dish of the day*

1. Aubergine; F. Moussaka
2. Tomato; D. Ketchup
3. Chickpea; J. Falafel
4. Avocado; E. Guacamole
5. Basil; B. Pesto
6. Potato; I. Rösti
7. Coffee beans; C. Cappuccino
8. Coconut; A. Korma
9. Almond; K. Frangipane
10. Onion; G. Bhaji
11. Chamomile; L. Tea
12. Cocoa; H. Mole sauce

Puzzle 11: *Crop rotation*

A. Brassicas: Broccoli, Brussel sprout, cauliflower, kale

B. Legumes: Broad bean, sugar snap, runner bean, mangetout

C. Onions: Chive, shallot, spring onions, leek

D. Cucurbits: Marrow, courgette, pumpkin, cucumber

E. Roots: Carrot, celery, parsnip, radish

Puzzle 12: Hanjie: *Shading by numbers*

Name of vegetable:

BUTTERNUT SQUASH

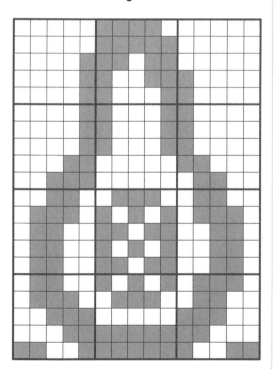

Puzzle 13: Multiple-choice: *Grow your own*

1. b) Coriander
2. d) Butt
3. b) Cloche
4. c) Kale
5. a) Courgette
6. b) Spears
7. a) Lemon
8. c) Drill
9. b) Rhubarb
10. b) Runners
11. a) Tubers
12. a) Nitrogen, phosphorus, potassium

Answers
Chapter Two: Horticultural Heroes

Puzzle 14: *Recommended reading*

1. *RURALIA Commoda* by Pietro Crescenzi
2. *Instructions in Gardening for LADIES* by Jane C Loudon
3. *The American GARDENER* by William Cobbett
4. *The WILD Garden* by William Robinson
5. *Wall and WATER Gardens* by Gertrude Jekyll
6. *We made a GARDEN* by Margery Fish
7. *The WELL-Tempered Garden* by Christopher Lloyd
8. *The DRY Garden* by Beth Chatto
9. *The EDUCATION of a Gardener* by Russell Page
10. *The TULIP* by Anna Pavord

Puzzle 15: *Taxonomic triangles*

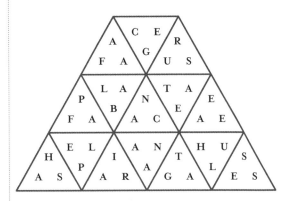

Puzzle 16: *Who am I?*

I am Lancelot 'Capability' Brown. The four parks pictured are (top to bottom): Stowe, Petworth Park, Burghley and Chatsworth.

Puzzle 17: *At the movies*

Below is the list in its new order

1. *Greenfingers* (2000); film C
2. *The Secret Garden* (1993); film A
3. *This Beautiful Fantastic* (2016); film F
4. *Serpent's Kiss* (1997); film B
5. *Dare to be Wild* (2015); film E
6. *A Little Chaos* (2014); film D

Puzzle 18: *Famous gardeners*

The garden is
SISSINGHURST.

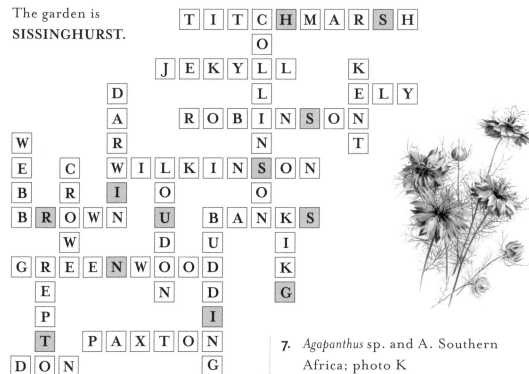

The crossword grid contains:

TITCHMARSH
COLL
JEKYLL   K
DLELY
AROBINSON
WRNT
WECWILKINSONSON
EBRION
BBROWNUBANKS
WUUI
GREENWOODDK
ENDG
P I
TPAXTON
DONG
N

Puzzle 19: *Where in the world?*

1. *Dahlia* sp. and C. Central America; photo I
2. *Pinus radiata* and F. Southwest North America; photo O
3. *Wollemia nobilis* and H. Blue Mountains of Australia; photo J
4. *Amorphophallus titanium* and D. Sumatra, Indonesia; photo M
5. *Dracunculus vulgaris* and B. Mediterranean; photo N
6. *Victoria amazonica* and E. South America; photo P
7. *Agapanthus* sp. and A. Southern Africa; photo K
8. *Araucaria araucana* and G. Central and southern Chile and western Argentina; photo L

Puzzle 20: Anagrams: *Horticulturally named celebrities*

1. KATE BUSH
2. HALLE BERRY
3. GUNS N ROSES
4. STONE ROSES
5. ROBERT PLANT
6. BOB FLOWERDEW
7. NIGELLA LAWSON
8. SEAN BEAN
9. GINGER ROGERS
10. THE CRANBERRIES

Puzzle 21: *Brick by brick*

The year in question is 1764.

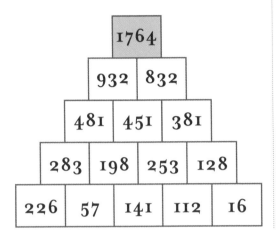

Puzzle 22: Mix and match: *Plant hunters*

1. David Douglas (B)
2. Robert Fortune (G)
3. Ernest Wilson (I)
4. William Lobb (D)
5. Alexander von Humboldt (F)
6. Joseph Banks (E)
7. Reginald Farrer (H)
8. Marianne North (A)
9. Archibald Menzies (J)
10. Frank Kingdon-Ward (C)

Puzzle 23: Word search: *Evergreens and conifers*

Pseudotsuga menziesii is the tree better known as Douglas fir.

I	H	U	P	I	N	U	S	S	A	B	I	N	I	A	N	A	C	I	K
I	B	N	M	I	O	U	H	P	T	E	F	P	R	Y	Y	L	R	W	K
S	O	F	Q	R	K	O	P	P	A	A	T	I	A	T	J	O	F	X	O
E	G	K	A	E	A	F	I	J	I	I	V	N	S	S	L	C	R	P	L
I	D	T	G	T	T	P	N	Q	D	I	U	U	O	U	V	I	P	U	M
Z	A	Y	S	L	S	D	U	Q	A	B	L	S	R	G	T	T	S	W	V
N	B	K	T	U	U	L	S	V	R	R	F	C	E	A	T	N	I	N	C
E	I	M	Q	O	N	A	L	I	S	X	C	O	D	H	K	O	S	P	C
M	E	T	D	C	E	B	A	T	U	X	W	N	N	E	Q	M	N	C	C
A	S	Q	B	S	V	I	M	F	N	Q	U	T	O	T	K	S	E	D	Q
G	A	C	W	U	S	E	B	Q	I	U	M	O	P	E	E	U	H	N	Y
U	M	L	N	N	E	S	E	P	P	D	D	R	S	R	D	N	C	E	I
S	A	S	X	I	I	P	R	U	V	V	X	T	U	O	W	I	T	X	Y
T	B	E	F	P	B	R	T	J	Z	U	U	A	N	P	E	P	I	B	U
O	I	L	D	M	A	O	I	U	J	Q	K	C	I	H	G	D	S	D	U
D	L	F	S	U	P	C	A	L	F	X	H	G	P	Y	A	O	A	B	Y
U	I	A	F	S	S	E	N	I	C	Z	S	G	M	L	D	D	E	M	C
E	S	I	Y	A	P	R	A	A	U	B	L	W	I	L	I	F	C	G	N
S	R	C	I	H	B	A	V	X	R	I	A	A	W	A	Q	D	I	N	H
P	M	A	X	A	B	I	E	S	G	R	A	N	D	I	S	N	P	F	I

Answers
Chapter Three: Wonderful Wildlife

Puzzle 24: *What am I?*

I am a woodpecker.

Puzzle 25: *Pollination game*

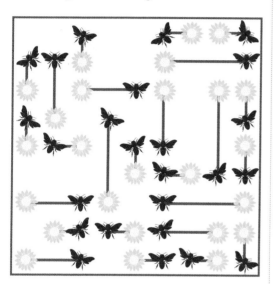

Puzzle 26: Multiple choice: *Garden visitors*

1. a) Apple
2. b) Vine weevil
3. d) Fox
4. c) Stow
5. c) Blackbird
6. d) Winter moth

Puzzle 27: Mix and match: *Plant eaters*

1. Deer (B)
2. Vine weevil (adult) (F)
3. Thrips (E)
4. Box tree caterpillar (G)
5. Glasshouse red spider mite (A)
6. Bean gall sawfly (C)
7. Gooseberry sawfly (D)
8. Currant blister aphid (H)

Puzzle 28: *Wildlife wordoku*

The answer is **BUTTERFLY.**

B	E	L	R	F	Y	U	A	T
A	U	Y	B	T	E	L	R	F
F	R	T	A	L	U	Y	E	B
R	Y	E	T	A	F	B	U	L
L	A	F	U	E	B	T	Y	R
T	B	U	L	Y	R	A	F	E
Y	L	R	E	B	A	F	T	U
E	F	B	Y	U	T	R	L	A
U	T	A	F	R	L	E	B	Y

Puzzle 29: Identity Parade:
Brilliantly beautiful butterflies

1. Red admiral
2. Purple emperor
3. Speckled wood
4. Small tortoiseshell
5. Comma
6. Brimstone

Puzzle 30: True or false?: *Busy Bees*

1. False
2. True
3. True
4. False
5. True
6. False
7. True
8. False
9. False
10. False

Puzzle 31: Hanjie: *Shading by numbers*
Name of visitor: **FROG**

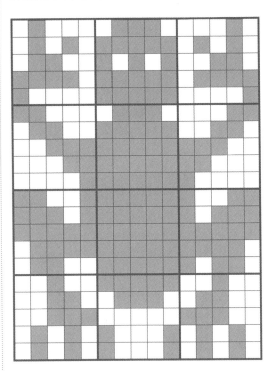

Puzzle 32: *Bird-spotting*

1. Buzzard; photo C
2. Red-tailed hawk; photo E
3. Merlin; photo H
4. Sparrowhawk; photo A
5. Kestrel; photo D
6. Great horned owl; photo F
7. Peregrine falcon; photo B
8. Barn owl; photo G

Puzzle 33: *Dormouse quest*

	I	2	🐭	2	3	🐭
2	🐭			2	🐭	🐭
			I		6	🐭
	🐭	2	I	🐭	🐭	🐭
I			I	2		3
I			2		2	🐭
🐭	2	🐭	2	🐭		I

Puzzle 34: Anagrams: *Cryptic critters*

1. RED SPIDER MITE
2. VINE WEEVIL
3. CODLING MOTH
4. WOOLLY APHID
5. NEMATODE
6. SNAIL
7. EARWIG
8. PHYLLOXERA

Puzzle 35: *Spot the difference*

Answers
Chapter Four: Botany Basics

Puzzle 36: *Flower power*

1. Heather; photo E
2. Pieris; photo B
3. Camellia; photo F
4. Enkianthus; photo C
5. Rhododendron; photo A
6. Vaccinium; photo D

Puzzle 37: *Climbing vines*

<table>
<tr><td>H</td><td>D</td><td>E</td><td>R</td><td>H</td><td>E</td><td>A</td></tr>
<tr><td>D</td><td>E</td><td>D</td><td>E</td><td>E</td><td>D</td><td></td></tr>
<tr><td>E</td><td>H</td><td>D</td><td>D</td><td>H</td><td>E</td><td>H</td></tr>
<tr><td>R</td><td>E</td><td>E</td><td>E</td><td>D</td><td>E</td><td></td></tr>
<tr><td>E</td><td>E</td><td>H</td><td>E</td><td>D</td><td>E</td><td>D</td></tr>
<tr><td>H</td><td>A</td><td>D</td><td>E</td><td>E</td><td>H</td><td></td></tr>
<tr><td>E</td><td>A</td><td>R</td><td>E</td><td>H</td><td>A</td><td></td></tr>
<tr><td>E</td><td>E</td><td>H</td><td>D</td><td>H</td><td>R</td><td></td></tr>
<tr><td>H</td><td>E</td><td>R</td><td>D</td><td>E</td><td>H</td><td></td></tr>
<tr><td>A</td><td>E</td><td>E</td><td>E</td><td>D</td><td>H</td><td></td></tr>
<tr><td>E</td><td>A</td><td>D</td><td>R</td><td>H</td><td>D</td><td>H</td></tr>
<tr><td>H</td><td>E</td><td>R</td><td>H</td><td>D</td><td>E</td><td></td></tr>
<tr><td>H</td><td>D</td><td>E</td><td>R</td><td>H</td><td>A</td><td>A</td></tr>
</table>

Puzzle 38: *Fun with fungi*

1. Oyster mushroom; photo D
2. Jelly ear; photo G
3. Giant puffball; photo H
4. Porcini; photo C
5. Chanterelle; photo F
6. Razor strop; photo E
7. Shaggy inkcap; photo A
8. Fly agaric; photo B

Puzzle 39: *Taxonomic Teaser*

1. Kingdom
2. Phylum/Division
3. Class
4. Order
5. Family
6. Genus
7. Species
8. Variety

Puzzle 40: *Anatomy of a flower*

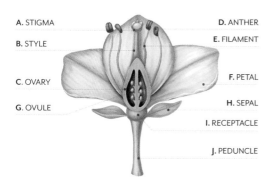

A. STIGMA

B. STYLE

C. OVARY

G. OVULE

D. ANTHER

E. FILAMENT

F. PETAL

H. SEPAL

I. RECEPTACLE

J. PEDUNCLE

The **pistil** is made up of the stigma, style and ovary.
The **stamen** is made up of the anther and the filament.

Puzzle 41: Word search: *Tree species*

The pictured tree is silver birch, *Betula pendula*.

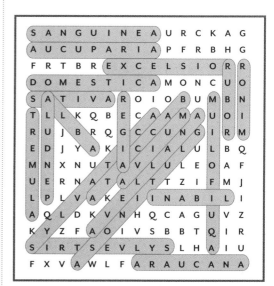

Puzzle 42: Anagrams: *Structural terms*

1. INTERNODE
2. STOMATA
3. RADICLE
4. PLUMULE
5. XYLEM
6. PHLOEM
7. EPIDERMIS
8. PALISADE

Puzzle 43: *All paired up*

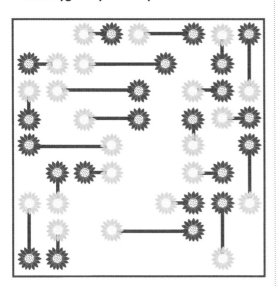

Puzzle 44: Multiple-choice: *Botany brain busters*

1. c) Sunflower
2. a) Flowering plants
3. a) Deciduous conifers
4. b) *Sequoia sempervirens*
5. b) Finely toothed
6. d) Covering of hair
7. b) Corks for wine bottles
8. b) Banana
9. c) Moss
10. a) Climber

Puzzle 45: Mix and match: *Happy families*

Rosaceae

3. *Prunus armeniaca*
5. *Cydonia oblonga*
12. *Eriobotrya japonica*
14. *Rubus chamaemorus*

Fabaceae

1. *Cicer arietinum*
7. *Tamarindus indica*
9. *Lotus corniculatus*
11. *Anthyllis vulneraria*

Orchidaceae

2. *Vanilla planifolia*
8. *Calypso bulbosa*
10. *Dactylorhiza viridis*
13. *Cymbidium goeringii*

Asteraceae

4. *Echinacea purpurea*
6. *Calendula officinalis*
15. *Taraxacum officinale*
16. *Achillea millefolium*

Answers
Chapter Five: Plant Identification

Puzzle 46: *Tall trees or amazing annuals?*

Trees

2. *Quercus robur*
3. *Sequoia sempervirens*
5. *Liquidambar styraciflua*
8. *Nothofagus dombeyi*
9. *Acer palmatum*
12. *Nyssa sylvatica*

Annuals

1. *Papaver commutatum*
4. *Limnanthes douglasii*
6. *Helianthus annus*
7. *Lathyrus odoratus*
10. *Orlaya grandiflora*
11. *Nigella damascena*

Puzzle 47: *Dot to dot*

The fruit is an apple.

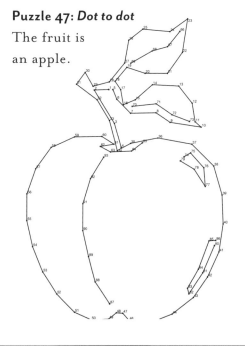

Puzzle 48: *Match the leaf to the plant*

1. *Liriodendron tulipifera*; photo B
2. *Monstera deliciosa*; photo L
3. *Jacobaea maritima*; photo G
4. *Fatsia japonica*; photo J
5. *Musa basjoo*; photo H
6. *Acanthus mollis*; photo C
7. *Dicksonia antartica*; photo E
8. *Acer palmatum*; photo A
9. *Vitis vinifera*; photo F
10. *Trachycarpus fortunei*; photo I
11. *Mimosa pudica*; photo K
12. *Cyclamen hederifolium*; photo D

Puzzle 49: Mix and match: *Bulb, rhizome, corm or tuber?*

Bulbs

2. Tulip
8. Hyacinth
11. Daffodil

Rhizomes

1. Iris
6. Canna lily
7. Ginger

Corms

3. Gladiolus
5. Crocus
12. Freesia

Tubers

4. Dahlia
9. Potato
10. Cyclamen

Puzzle 50: *The germination game*

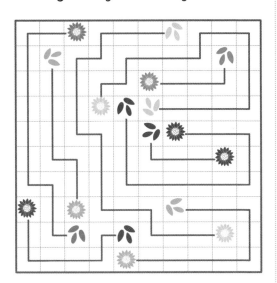

Puzzle 51: Mix and match: *Bulbtastic*

1. *Nerine bowdenii* (C)
2. *Scilla siberica* (J)
3. *Crocus vernus* (H)
4. *Narcissus poeticus* (F)
5. *Galanthus nivalis* (E)
6. *Anemone blanda* (D)
7. *Hyacinthus orientalis* (G)
8. *Allium sphaerocephalon* (B)
9. *Lilium lancifolium* (A)
10. *Tulipa linifolia* (I)

Puzzle 52: *Deadly dozen*

The picture image is 1. *Digitalis purpurea*, aka foxglove.

1. Deadly (foxglove)
2. Edible (wild cabbage)
3. Deadly (deadly nightshade)
4. Edible (leek)
5. Deadly (monkshood)
6. Deadly (castor oil plant)
7. Edible (radish)
8. Deadly (common yew)
9. Edible (beet)
10. Deadly (hemlock)
11. Edible (romaine lettuce)
12. Edible (runner bean)

Puzzle 53: *Wordoku*

The plant family is
ASTERACEAE.

A	M	O	R	T	D	E	L	C	S
E	S	D	C	L	T	M	A	R	O
D	A	T	S	O	E	R	C	L	M
R	L	C	E	M	S	O	D	T	A
T	O	E	A	R	C	D	M	S	L
M	D	S	L	C	A	T	O	E	R
O	R	A	T	E	L	C	S	M	D
L	C	M	D	S	R	A	E	O	T
S	E	R	O	D	M	L	T	A	C
C	T	L	M	A	O	S	R	D	E

Puzzle 54: *Coming up roses*

White roses

'Iceberg'; photo A

'Alba'; photo F

'Claire Austin'; photo K

'Desdemona'; photo G

Red roses

'Wilhelm'; photo B

'Crimson Shower'; photo J

'Darcey Bussell'; photo H

'Trumpeter'; photo E

Yellow roses

'Arthur Bell'; photo C

'Canary Bird'; photo D

'Graham Thomas'; photo I

'Charlotte'; photo L

Puzzle 55: *Mustard mayhem*

1. CABBAGE
2. CAULIFLOWER
3. KALE
4. BROCCOLI
5. KOHLRABI
6. TURNIP
7. RADISH
8. ROCKET
9. SEA KALE
10. WASABI

Puzzle 56: *Buried berries*

●	1		●	●	2	●
2		2		2		2
●		●		1	2	●
2	3	1	2		●	2
●			2	●	3	2
3	●	●		2		●
●	4	●	3	●	2	1

Answers
Chapter Six: Gardening Techniques

Puzzle 57: *Which technique?*

The answer is A. The other techniques shown are:

E. Chip bud

F. Layering a shoot

C. Collecting seed

B. Potting on a plant

D. Pricking out

Puzzle 58: *Field work*

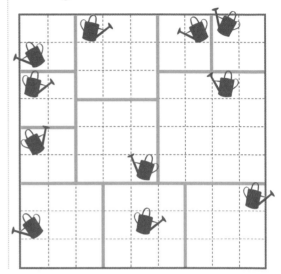

Puzzle 59: *Peat-free compost*

I	K	Q	X	P	B	B	L	H	L	V	E	B	Z	F	Q	T	H	Q	L
V	W	W	E	L	V	A	T	O	F	C	I	W	J	W	B	S	N	P	Y
D	Q	G	X	K	P	G	A	R	F	R	H	Q	U	A	L	Y	C	C	Y
M	A	K	Z	A	B	L	K	T	Q	F	J	E	G	U	L	I	Y	J	J
I	B	Q	P	U	Z	J	F	I	X	C	N	T	N	C	O	W	Q	L	Y
X	M	O	R	O	F	M	V	C	I	O	U	O	W	P	O	F	A	F	E
S	W	L	E	E	G	A	O	U	B	C	P	Y	O	E	W	Q	M	I	L
Y	O	Z	R	T	Y	P	D	L	U	O	I	B	O	R	E	Q	Y	L	M
T	W	Z	B	I	O	N	U	T	I	N	K	U	D	L	N	D	F	N	G
O	Q	M	I	L	B	C	P	U	K	U	W	N	C	I	O	H	K	K	K
H	Y	S	F	U	Q	Q	W	R	S	T	A	K	H	T	T	A	V	B	F
E	M	W	D	C	R	D	T	A	B	F	V	N	I	E	S	V	T	Z	Z
Y	W	A	O	I	J	F	W	L	L	I	S	G	P	W	D	H	S	M	U
I	T	G	O	M	O	J	K	G	U	B	K	H	P	S	R	M	U	N	L
A	H	O	W	R	U	Y	H	R	N	R	B	T	I	V	D	B	D	D	D
Q	W	D	Q	E	U	M	U	I	L	E	R	B	N	Y	K	N	W	N	X
J	H	I	H	V	V	Y	M	T	I	G	I	L	G	E	D	N	A	S	M
F	C	L	F	X	S	K	V	Z	J	D	Q	K	S	K	D	J	S	Y	U
Q	O	E	O	K	D	G	O	V	H	J	O	J	C	Z	N	I	N	S	T
C	N	F	Y	B	F	Z	U	V	L	O	O	W	K	C	O	R	P	K	L

Puzzle 60: *Lawn loop*

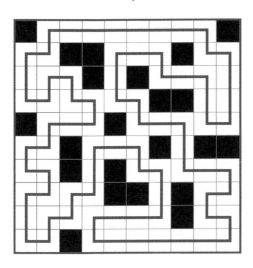

Puzzle 61: Hanjie: *Shading by numbers*

Name of fruit: TOMATO

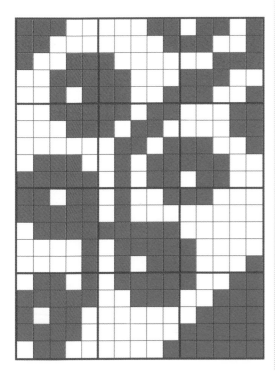

Puzzle 62: Compost conundrum: *Green or brown?*

6. Fallen leaves
8. Shredded paper
9. Wood chippings
12. Shredded cardboard boxes

Puzzle 63: *Fences*

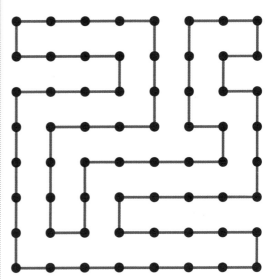

Puzzle 64: *The cutting edge*

1. ESPALIER
2. FEATHERED TREE
3. MAIDEN WHIP
4. OBLIQUE CORDON
5. UPRIGHT CORDON
6. STANDARD
7. MULTI-STEMMED TREE
8. OPEN-CENTRE GOBLET
9. PLEACHED
10. FAN

Puzzle 65: Anagrams:
Techniques with a twist

1. PRUNING
2. DIGGING
3. MULCHING
4. STAKING
5. PLANTING
6. WEEDING
7. HOEING
8. RAKING
9. MOWING
10. SOWING

Puzzle 66: *Yearly rotation*

1 ↓	4 ↘	7 ↘	6 ←
9 ↘	12 ↓	3 ↖	8 ←
14 ↘	13 ←	11 ↖	5 ↑
2 ↗	15 →	10 ↑	16

Puzzle 67: Mix and match: *The green grass of home*

1. Half moon; photo K
2. Strimmer; photo B
3. Cylinder mower; photo E
4. Rotary mower; photo D
5. Edging shears; photo L
6. Aerator spikes; photo G
7. Weeding tool; photo F
8. Turfing iron; photo A
9. Spreader; photo I
10. Roller; photo C
11. Leaf rake; photo J
12. Scarifier machine; photo H

Puzzle 68: Multiple-choice: *Gardening techniques*

1. a) Secateurs
2. b) A roller on the back of a mower
3. b) No dig
4. c) Sucker
5. d) Cutting branches
6. a) Layering
7. a) Companion planting
8. b) Cloud pruning
9. b) Drying out damp soil
10. d) Etiolation

Answers

Chapter Seven: Gardens Around the World

Puzzle 69: Mix and match:
Location finder

1. Royal Botanic Gardens of Sydney, Australia (D)
2. Ryoan-ji, Kyoto, Japan (F)
3. Jardim Botânico, Rio de Janeiro, Brazil (C)
4. Villa d'Este Gardens, Tivoli, Italy (E)
5. Kirstenbosch, Cape Town, South Africa (A)
6. Majorelle Garden, Marrakech, Morocco (B)

The pictured gardens are (top to bottom)

· Majorelle Garden
· Ryoan-ji
· Villa d'Este Gardens

Puzzle 70: *Palatial spaces*

1. PETERHOF, Russia
2. ALHAMBRA, Spain
3. DROTTNINGHOLM, Sweden
4. HAMPTON COURT, England
5. CASTEL GANDOLFO, Italy
6. SANSSOUCI, Germany
7. MUGHAL GARDEN, India
8. ROYAL GREENHOUSES OF LAEKEN, Belgium

Puzzle 71: *Triangle conundrum*

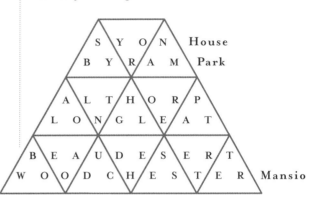

Puzzle 72: *Where am I?*
Answer: I am Keukenhof in the Netherlands.

Puzzle 73: *Spot the difference*

Puzzle 74: *Garden maze*

Puzzle 75: Word search:
Gardens of Versailles

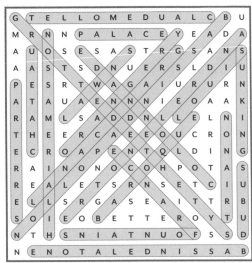

Puzzle 76: *City park identifier*

1. Central Park, New York; photo C
2. Tiergarten, Berlin; photo B
3. Jardin du Luxembourg, Paris; photo G
4. Lumpini Park, Bangkok; photo H
5. Hyde Park, London; photo E
6. Stanley Park, Vancouver; photo A
7. El Retiro, Madrid; photo D
8. Tivoli Gardens, Copenhagen; photo F

Puzzle 77: Anagrams: *Garden styles through time*

1. GARDENESQUE
2. PICTURESQUE
3. FRENCH BAROQUE
4. BYZANTINE
5. HELLENISTIC
6. PERSIAN
7. MODERNIST
8. NATURALISTIC
9. MESOPOTAMIAN
10. ENGLISH LANDSCAPE MOVEMENT

Pictured: Persian

Puzzle 78 (see also below):

Word fit: *World gardens*

The four featured gardens are:

A. Hidcote
B. Villa D'este, Tivoli
C. Nong Nooch Tropical Botanical Garden
D. Powerscourt Gardens

Answers
Chapter Eight: Garden Features and Design

Puzzle 79: *Muddled methods*

1. MITTLEIDER METHOD
2. BIODYNAMIC
3. PERMACULTURE
4. HYDROPONICS
5. ORGANIC
6. AQUAPONICS
7. NO DIG
8. COMPANION

Puzzle 80: *Up the garden path*

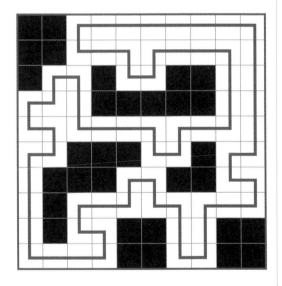

Puzzle 81: *Sustainable gardening*

1. HUGELKULTUR
2. RAISED BED
3. STRAW BALE
4. CONTAINER
5. SQUARE FOOT
6. LASAGNE

Puzzle 82: *Building bridges*

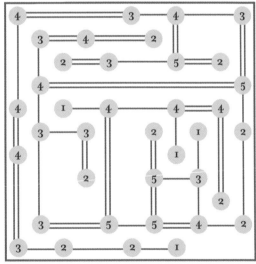

Puzzle 83: Multiple choice:
Garden features

1. a) Parterre
2. b) Ha ha
3. d) Folly
4. a) Knot garden
5. b) Dovecote
6. d) Potager
7. a) A dewy path
8. a) Coppice
9) c) Grotto
10) a) Allée

Puzzle 84: *Sunshine or shade?*
Sunshine

1. *Lavandula angustifolia*
6. *Sanvitalia procumbens*
7. *Echinops ritro*
9. *Citrus × aurantiifolia*
10. *Lantana camara*

Shade

2. *Hedera helix*
3. *Iris foetidissima*
4. *Eranthis hyemalis*
5. *Anemone nemorosa*
8. *Brunnera macrophylla*

Pictured: *Anemone nemorosa*

Puzzle 85: *Garden folly*

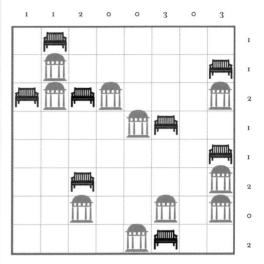

Puzzle 86: *Garden installations*

1. Barbecue
2. Decking
3. Water feature
4. Patio
5. Seating area
6. Terrace
7. Wormery
8. Water butt
9. Compost heap
10. Cold frames

Puzzle 87: Mix and match:

Garden planting

1. Fernery; B. *Athyrium filix-femina*
2. Alpine bed; H. *Lewisia longipetala*
3. Fruit garden; C. *Malus domestica*
4. Water feature in conservatory; F. *Nelumbo nucifera*
5. Pinetum; E. *Pinus sylvestris*
6. Herbaceous border; A. *Delphinium elatum*
7. Orangery; G. *Citrus × paradisi*
8. Vegetable bed; D. *Lactuca sativa*

Puzzle 88: *Spot the difference*

Puzzle 89: *Past masters*

John Tradescant the younger; 1608–62

André Le Nôtre; 1613–1700

Peter Joseph Lenné; 1789–1866

Frederick Law Olmsted; 1822–1903

Gertrude Jekyll; 1843–1932

Norah Lindsay; 1866–1948

Vita Sackville-West; 1892–1962

Brenda Colvin; 1897–1981

Herta Hammerbacher; 1900–85

Geoffrey Jellicoe; 1900–96

Thomas Church; 1902–78

Pechère René; 1908–2002

Roberto Burle Marx; 1909–94

Corajoud Michel; 1937–2014

John Brookes; 1933–2018

Pictured: Sackville-West (A), Olmsted (B) and Tradescant the younger (C)

Answers

Chapter Nine: Tales from the Potting Shed

Puzzle 90: *Tools to test you*

1. DIBBER
2. PROPAGATOR
3. LOPPERS
4. EDGING SHEARS
5. SECATEURS
6. ROTAVATOR
7. WHEELBARROW
8. SPRING TINE RAKE
9. RIDE ON
10. WATERING CAN
11. ONION HOE
12. DAISY GRUBBER

Puzzle 91: *Planting out*

Fernery

4. *Asplenium scolopendrium*
7. *Athyrium niponicum*
11. *Dryopteris filix-mas*
12. *Osmunda regalis*
14. *Matteuccia struthiopteris*
15. *Dicksonia antarctica*

Conifer glade

2. *Cupressocyparis leylandii*
6. *Abies koreana*
10. *Thuja plicata*
13. *Chamaecyparis lawsoniana*
17. *Cryptomeria japonica*
24. *Taxus baccata*

Herbaceous perennial border

5. *Echinops ritro*
16. *Sedum spectabile*
19. *Echinacea purpurea*
21. *Verbena bonariensis*
22. *Alchemilla mollis*
25. *Hemerocallis fulva*

Deciduous trees for autumn colour

1. *Amelanchier lamarckii*
3. *Nyssa sylvatica*
20. *Quercus rubra*
27. *Acer palmatum*
28. *Cercidiphyllum japonicum*
29. *Liquidambar styraciflua*

In the pond (aquatic plants)

8. *Hippuris vulgaris*
9. *Callitriche stagnalis*
18. *Hottonia palustris*
26. *Ranunculus hederaceus*
23. *Hydrocharis morsus-ranae*
30. *Nymphaea alba*

Puzzle 92: *Spot the difference*

Puzzle 93: *Perfect lawn wordoku*

The hidden tool is **SCARIFIER.**

S	E	I	F	R	L	A	T	C
F	C	T	S	A	I	E	R	L
L	R	A	T	E	C	S	I	F
I	L	C	R	S	T	F	A	E
T	A	F	L	I	E	R	C	S
E	S	R	A	C	F	T	L	I
C	F	L	E	T	R	I	S	A
R	I	S	C	F	A	L	E	T
A	T	E	I	L	S	C	F	R

Puzzle 94: *Beans*

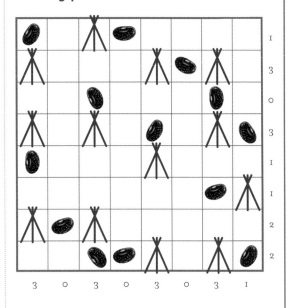

Puzzle 95: Anagrams: *Potting shed staples*

1. STRING
2. SEED PACKETS
3. FLOWERPOTS
4. TROWEL
5. SECATEURS
6. FERTILIZER
7. WATERING CAN
8. POTTING TABLE

Puzzle 96: *Wheelbarrow path*

I ↘	7 ↘	5 ↙	4 ←
13 ↓	6 ↑	3 ↗	9 ↙
11 →	12 ↖	2 ↑	8 ↑
14 →	10 ↖	15 →	16

Puzzle 97: *Propagation methods*

1. Division; photo G
2. Pricking out; photo E
3. Hardwood cutting; photo A
4. Direct sowing; photo B
5. Budding; photo D
6. Leaf cutting; photo H
7. Heel cutting; photo F
8. Offset propagation; photo C

Puzzle 98: *What am I?*

I am a besom.

Puzzle 99: *Tilling the soil*

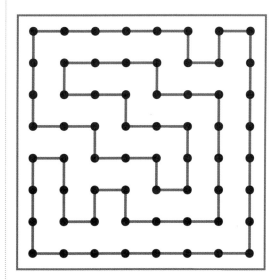

Puzzle 100: Mix and match:

Fit for the task

1. Pruning a hedge; E. Hand shears
2. Weeding; D. Flame gun
3. Cutting long grass; C. Scythe
4. Creating a straight line to mark a border; F. String
5. Loosening the surface of the soil; A. Three-pronged cultivator
6. Cutting a branch; B. Pruning saw

Puzzle 101: *Dot to dot*

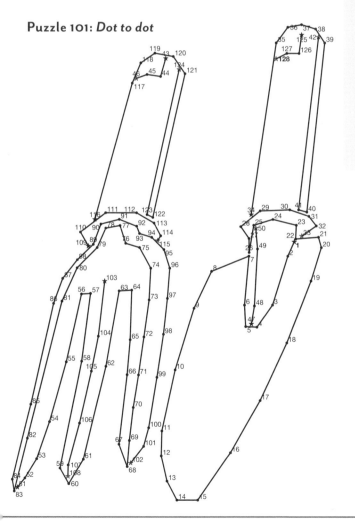

ABOUT THE AUTHORS

Simon Akeroyd is the author of *RHS Gardening School* and the *RHS Allotment Handbook and Planner* (both Mitchell Beazley). He was previously a Garden Manager for the Royal Horticultural Society, and worked at both RHS Wisley and Harlow Carr.

Dr Gareth Moore is a puzzle expert who has authored numerous bestselling books, including the enduringly popular *Ordnance Survey Puzzle Book* and *Mindfulness Puzzle Book*. He would like to thank Laura Jayne Ayres for her help in preparing many of the puzzles in this book.

Picture Credits

Alamy: 12 Francisco de Zurbarán; 27 Stocktrek Images; 34 (A) BFA, (B) United Archives GMBH, (C) Maximum Film, (D) Moviestore Collection, (E) Cinematic Collection, (F) Lifestyle Pictures; 49 Heritage Image Partnership; 53 Science History Images; 54–55, 106 Sunny Celeste; 67, 174tl Andrea Danti; 89 (B) Helen Cowles, (J) Martin Hughes-Jones; 94 (C) PURPLE MARBLES GARDEN; 94 (F), 107 (A) Dorling Kindersley ltd; 107 (E) Pollen Photos; 108 ClassicStock; 109tl Emilio Ereza; 118, 183 Historic Illustrations; 125 Art Directors & TRIP; 132 (6) Deborah Vernon; 133 M&N; 135 North Wind Picture Archives; 141, 187 Quagga Media. **Botanicalillustrations. org:** 31; 32; 47t; 70, 174bl; 73; 74, 175b; 78tl; 82tr; 86; 91; 148; 149tr; 149tl; 149bl; 152; 153; 189b; 157 (D), 157 (F). **Mary Evans Picture Library:** 26 Classic Stock/H. Armstrong Roberts; 147 Illustration by AFM, c. 1891. Getty Images: 42t DigitalVision Vectors.

Photoshop: 123 (H) Lepneva Irina. **Shutterstock:** Front cover mamita; 8–9 Bibit Mateng; 11tr Potapov Alexander; 11b Trigubova Irina; 13 Balora; 14 (A) Stuarts Photography, (B) Petro Hz, (C) Gala_Kan; 15 (D) demm28, (E) Volodymyr Nikitenko, (F) Hortimages, (G) Peter Turner Photography, (H) Patnaree Asavacharanitich, (I) Max_555, (J) D K Grove, (K) MM7, (L) LSP EM; 17bl Randrei, 17bc DN BR, 17br Eroshka; 18 (A) bergamont, (B) Brookgardener, (C) Ewa Saks, (D) Wasanajai, (E) Svetliy, (F) Le Do; 19 (G) Sergiy Akhundov, (H) Bahadir Yeniceri, (I) Hari Mahidhar, (J) PosiNote, (K) nnattalli, (L) Jiang Hongyan; 28–29 Lisla; 33t Skowronec 33ct Mr Mcfly; 33cb Goncalo Telo; 33b mountaintreks; 36–37 world map Tanarch; 37 (I) Alex Manders, (J) simona pavan, (K) Dina Einstein, (L) gkmndesign, (M) Lexwanto, (N) Natalia van D, (O) Peter Turner Photography, (P) Martin Fowler; 39 Alesikka; 44–45 Olga Korneeva; 46 Alena Paletskayer; 47, 170 (bee) Olga _Angelloz, (flower) Yamurchik; 50 (A) Olya Maximenko, (B) Niki Florin, (C) Tricky_Shark, (D) Boreiko, (E) Cr. E. Srinivas (F) D. Kucharski K. Kucharska, (G) Nancy Beijersberben, (H) Orest lyzhechka; 56 (A) mycteria, (B) Harry Collins Photography, (C) Ondrej, (D) Milan Zygmunt, (E) Ian Duffield, (F) Theresa Lauria, (G) duangnapa, (H) John C Evans; 60–61, 66, 92–93, 162–163 mamita; 62 (A) Natalia van D, (B) Gabriela Beres, (C) marineke thissen, (D) HelloSSTK, (E) AnnaNel, (F) Ole Shoener; 63c Alesikka; 65 (A) SciPhi.tv, (B) Arie v.d. Wolde, (C) Maksim Safaniuk, (D) Jennifer Wharton, (E) arazu, (F) nitr, (G) Jaroslav Machacek, (G) Henri Koskinen; 68–69 Valerii_M; 71, 83, 175t, 177t (sunflower) Yamurchik; 71b, 83b, 100b, 101b, 159b Uncle Leo; 72 (A) Mabeline, (B) Vo Thi Thao Lan, (C) Skrypnykov Dmytro, (D) CreativeMedia.org.uk; 75 (1) Catherine_P, (2) guentermanaus, (3) Irina Borsuchenko, (4) Audrey Wilson 1, (5) darksoul72, (6) Wolfen, (7) M.INTAKUM, (8) Mika Heikkinen, (9) LIhor Hvozdetskyi, (10) Coulanges, (11) Nahhana, (12) traction, (13) goriyan, (14) rbkomar, (15) Keikona, (16) Tatiana Volgutova; 76–77

Yevheniia Lytvynovych; 80 (A) Madlen, (B) Marinodenisenko, (C) Furiarossa, (D) Erik Agar, (E) Alagz, (F) Dmytro Furman; 81 (G) Tamara Kulikova, (H) Doikanoy, (I) Gardens by Design (J) shepherdsatellite, (L) trytrle, (M) Sozina Kseniia; 82 (bulb) ArtMari, (rhizome) Sasha_Ivanova, (corm, tuber) Kazakova Maryia; 83, 177t (seeds) Dn Br; 84tl Diana Taliun; 84br Natalia van D; 85 (2) Elena Tratsevskaya, (3) Iva Vagnerova, (4) S.O.E., (5) Greens and Blues, (6) Insa Mlodzinski, (7) Anongluckruttana, (8) lovelypeace, (9) svf74, (10) Sergey V Kalyakin; 89 (A) Bonnie Taylor Barry, (C) Sergey V Kalyakin, (D) Whiteaster, (E) zzz555zzz, (F) Veranika Dzik, (G) Gary Matuschka, (H) Sergey Bezgodov, (I) lenel. garden, (K) Sergey V Kalyakin, (L) Monika Pa; 94 (A) Lynsey Grosfield, (B) K.Kargona, (D) Viktor Sergeevich, (E) okan celik; 95, 179 (watering can) nemlaza; 95b bmf-foto.de; 96 Fancy Tapis; 97, 119, 151 Ann in the uk; 98 Kazakova Maryia; 100 (wooden post) alyaBigJoy; 105 ArtMari; 107 (B) Vadym Zaitsev, (C) Dean Clarke, (D) Vitalliy, (F) Sherwood, (G) LaNataly, (H) Jerome.Romme, (I) The Toidi, (J) Ozgur Coskun, (K) Stacey Newman, (L) JaneHYork; 110–111 Net Vector; 113t Tim de Waardt; 113c Vanessa Roca; 113b Sina Ettmer Photography; 117 Sultanyono Tan; 122 (A) poemnist, (B) Novikov Aleksey, (C) Maglara, (D) Catarina Belova; 123 (E) pcruciatti, (F) Denis Aminev, (G) PHOTOCREO Michal Bednarek; 127 (A) Mo W, (B) lapas77, (C) Panwasin seemala, (D) agsaz; 128–129 Mirexon; 131, 137b VETOCHKA; 132 (1) NayaDadara, (2) Crowing Hen, (3) Miriam Doerr Martin Frommherz, (4) Jorge Salcedo, (5) Nura M; 137, 186 (gazebo) Design_Stock7; 138 (1) Ismiths, (2) sanddebeautheil, (3) Red Pagoda, (4) Paul Maguire; 139 (5) Shahar Shabtai, (6) Olga Gavrilova, (7) HollyHarry, (8) Delovely Pics, (9) JurateBuiviene, (10) AC Rider; 144–145 Alexandra Iva; 150, 189t Olga Korneeva; 156 (A) Maverick76, (B) ch_ch; 157 (C) Firn, (E) Irina Starikova3432, (G) VH-studio, (H) johan Kusuma; 160 (A) Bozena Fulawka, (B) Serg64, (C) Peyker, (D) Phichai, (E) Martin Darley, (F) Ruslan Khismatov; 172t basel101658; 186 (bench) Dn Br. **Wikimedia Commons:** 1, 130; 4, 68t, 174tr; 5b, 78b; 7, 78br; 10; 16t; 16b Wotto Wilhelm Thome; 20; 21; 22l Rawpixel ltd; 22r; 23; 24–25, 166br; 30; 35 and 168; 38; 40; 41; 42b; 48; 50t; 51; 52, 171; 52, 171; 52, (3, 4, 5, 6) 90; 57; 58; 59 and 172b; 59; 63tl, tr, br, 173; 65; 66 (Lineaus); 79; 87; 88, 178; 90b; 100t; 102, 182; 103; 104; 109b; 112; 114; 115; 116; 120; 121; 124; 130; 132t; 134; 136; 138t; 140; 142; 146; 149br; 154; 155; 156tl; 158; 161; 191.

Every effort has been made to credit the copyright holders of the images used in this book. The publisher apologises for any unintentional omissions or errors and will insert the appropriate acknowledgment to any companies or individuals in subsequent editions of the work.